TOUR

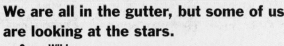

> We are all in the gutter, but some of us are looking at the stars.
> —Oscar Wilde

ACKNOWLEDGMENTS

A special note of gratitude to my parents, Theresa and Frank Turtu, who still get as excited by my work as I do. My thanks to Tom, Matt, and Donald (discussing movies with you has been just as much fun as watching them), and to Robert for finally dragging me into the technical age. Thanks to Tina Hummel, Katherine Mericale, Vic Gupta, and Marge Schictanz for riding to the rescue; to Jim Zicopula, Alan Levine, Denis de Wulf, and Gordon Kalisch for their kindness and patience as I searched for the perfect images to tell my story; to John Cocchi at JC Archives for finding just the right photo each time I ran into a brick wall; to Jeffrey Lyons and Leonard Maltin for their time and kind words; and to everyone at Collectors Press, especially Richard Perry, Jennifer Weaver-Neist, Kathryn Juergens, Laura Bartroff, and Lisa M. Douglass who came to appreciate the "girls" and my fascination with them.

My sincere appreciation to the legendary Angie Dickinson, who pulled the entire project together with her participation and kind support.

Lastly, a special thanks to the actresses who appear within these pages. I remember a shy young boy who watched your images flicker across a small black-and-white television set many years ago. Collectively you warmed his heart and touched his soul. The boy grew up, and I really like the person he's become. Thanks for making the journey with me.

LOBBY CARD

A vineyard owner's cheating bride (Diana Dors, 1931–34) and his handsome young foreman (Tom Tryon) conduct an illicit affair which leads to murder in *The Unholy Wife* (RKO, 1957), a failed attempt to turn the British Dors into a great American sex symbol.

BAD GIRLS

TONY TURTU

FILM FATALES, SIRENS, AND MOLLS

COLLECTORS PRESS

Book Design: Lisa M. Douglass, Collectors Press, Inc.
Project Manager: Jennifer Weaver-Neist
Editors: Jade Chan and Julie Steigerwaldt

Library of Congress Cataloging-in-Publication Data

Turtu, Tony
  Bad girls : film fatales, sirens, and molls / Tony Turtu.-- 1st American ed.
    p.   cm.
  Includes index.
  ISBN 1-933112-03-4 (hardcover : alk. paper)
  1. Femmes fatales in motion pictures. 2. Women in motion pictures.
  I. Title.
  PN1995.9.F44T87 2005
  791.43'6522--dc22
                              2004025507

Printed in Singapore

9 8 7 6 5 4 3 2 1

Collectors Press books are available at special discounts for bulk purchases, premiums, and promotions. Special editions, including personalized inserts or covers, and corporate logos, can be printed in quantity for special purposes. For further information contact: Special Sales, Collectors Press, Inc., P.O. Box 230986, Portland, OR 97281. Toll free: 1-800-423-1848.

For a free catalog write: Collectors Press, Inc., P.O. Box 230986, Portland, OR 97281. Toll free: 1-800-423-1848 or visit our website at: collectorspress.com.

End papers:
(PUBLICITY STILL) With practically no budget to speak of, Edgar G. Ulmer directed the now classic film noir *Detour* (PRC, 1945), starring Ann Savage (1921–) as one of the screen's cheapest and cruelest females (true to her last name). When down-on-his-luck Al (Tom Neal) offers the black-mailing Vera (Ann Savage) a ride, his life will never be the same. The no-frills production only added to the gritty atmosphere, making *Detour* a minor masterpiece and Ann a pulp legend.
(JC Archives)

Page 1:
In Jacques Tourneur's *Out of the Past* (RKO, 1947), Jane Greer (1924–2001), as backstabbing Kathie Moffett, created a role by which many future femme fatales were measured. Jane was at her slinkiest (not to mention her most rotten) in this brilliant film noir, considered to be one of the finest by aficionados of the genre. She appeared in the 1983 remake, *Against All Odds*, this time playing the mother of the character she portrayed in the original.
(JC Archives)

Page 5:
SCENE STILL. Ruth Roman (1922–99), *The Window* (RKO, 1949). (JC Archives)

Jacket flap (left):
ONE SHEET POSTER. Anita Ekberg (1931–), *The Cobra* (A.I.P., 1968).

Jacket flap (right):
LOBBY CARD. Carol Ohmart (1927–), *The Scarlet Hour* (Paramount, 1956).

PORTRAIT STILL

The story of the infamous Dalton Brothers of the old West got a Hollywood makeover in *The Dalton Girls* (United Artists, 1957) which offers four distantly related dames taking over for the boys on a frontier crime wave. Merry Anders (1932–), pictured here, headed the beguiling band of outlaw women in what was just one of the nearly fifty films (mostly Bs) she appeared in. (JC Archives)

CONTENTS

INTRODUCTION

A DOE-eyed farm girl in pigtails valiantly endures a blinding rainstorm while searching for her missing colt; a young schoolmarm in a gingham prairie skirt helps her sickly grandfather save his ranch from cattle rustlers; a fair English lass works on her needlepoint while she stoically awaits her fiancé's return from battle. Sorry, kids, not in this book! As the images in this book clearly attest, this is a celebration of the wicked, the wayward, and the wanton, and of the actresses (and lesser-known starlets, featured players, et al) who gave those celluloid sinners their oomph. Silent pictures gave birth to the mother of all "bad girls," known as the vamp, a derivation of the word "vampire." Popularized in 1914 by actress Theda Bara (among several

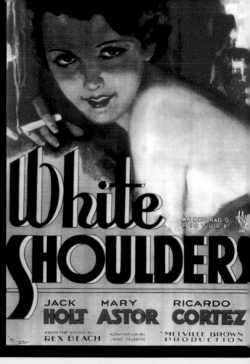

WINDOW CARD

White SHOULDERS

JACK **HOLT**   MARY **ASTOR**   RICARDO **CORTEZ**

FROM THE STORY BY
REX BEACH
ADAPTATION BY
JANE MURFIN
MELVILLE BROWN
PRODUCTION

AN RKO RADIO PICTURE

That provocative stare, the curl of cigarette smoke, and the hint of exposed skin (*gasp!*) was enough to fill the seats when *White Shoulders* (RKO, 1931), starring Mary Astor (1906–87) was released. Mary's sometimes incendiary private life, rife with scandal (her X-rated diary was introduced into evidence during a 1936 custody hearing), nearly derailed her career, but when she returned to the screen she proved to be more popular than ever, especially as cynical, grasping femme fatales. Mary won an Oscar for Best Supporting Actress in 1941 for *The Great Lie*, and was at her baddest as a rotten tomato in *The Maltese Falcon* that same year.

SCENE STILL

Joan Bennett (1910–90) made four films under the direction of Fritz Lang that have come to define the bleak and desperate world of film noir. In *Scarlet Street* (Universal, 1945) Joan is at her most venal as a coldhearted blackmailer who preys on a lonely henpecked man (Edward G. Robinson) who falls for her. Dan Duryea (seated) played her abusive partner in crime in a film that helped establish Joan as a big screen femme fatale. The three other Lang/Bennett joint ventures were *Man Hunt*, *The Woman in the Window*, and *The Secret Beyond the Door*. (JC Archives)

others), vamp came to represent cold, exotic, and unscrupulous destroyers of men in scores of melodramas. So impressionable were audiences of the day that picture-goers were seen kicking publicity stills of Theda after showings of her photoplays. Once a young mother threatened to call the police when her child spoke to La Bara, as she was called, on the sidewalks of New York! Thankfully the public became more comfortable with the representation of loose women on screen, and savvy studios realized there was gold in those gold diggers! After the movies learned how to talk, there was usually a blonde (OK, sometimes she was a redhead) who knew her way around a wisecrack. Some of these dames could say more with a sneer than most actresses could say with an entire page of dialogue. This was especially true of the Depression-era Hollywood of the 1930s and beyond, where a sexually charged innuendo delivered

MARIA MONTEZ
JON HALL
SABU
in
COBRA WOMAN
in TECHNICOLOR
with
EDGAR BARRIER
Lois Collier Mary Nash
and
LON CHANEY
as Hava

SPECTACULAR CAST OF THOUSANDS!

In *Cobra Woman* (Universal, 1944) twin sisters (one cold and bloodthirsty, the other kind and sympathetic) battle each other for the right to rule their island kingdom. This foolishness was heightened by the amusingly wooden performance of its star, Maria Montez (1920–51) in a dual role, proving once and for all that one Maria was bad enough but two was a sensory overload! (JC Archives)

through a veil of cigarette smoke was a clear distinction between the bad girl and her less-daring counterpart. Encompassing film noir femme fatales, brassy blondes, juvenile delinquents, and their foreign sisters, this book shines a spotlight (or would an interrogation lamp be more fitting?) on several genres of filmmaking where these mantraps flourished. So let's thumb a ride (preferably in a 1957 Pontiac) with a steamy assortment of chorines, dance hall hostesses, adulteresses, strippers, she-devils, and fallen women. It won't be a dull trip, especially with these gals at the wheel! Were these women repellent? Sometimes. Redeemable? Yes, occasionally. Alluring? Definitely. Even when a bad girl wreaked havoc on some poor guy, didn't we secretly applaud her less-than-exemplary behavior? Certainly that was half the fun of watching the movie in the first place. If she was rotten-to-the-core, it was all the better. As the ad copy on a long forgotten B picture once proudly boasted, "She was the kind of mistake a man can make only once." Somehow we knew that the film's hero would never be quite the same again, and, happily, neither would we.

Tony Turtu
September 2004

PUBLICITY STILL

The mythology of silent movie actress Theda Bara (1890–1955) was sold to a gullible public as the love child (born beneath the shadow of the Sphinx, no less) of a French artist and an Egyptian dancer, when in reality Theda was born in Ohio and grew up in a small apartment above her father's tailor shop. It was also suggested that her name was an ancient anagram for "Arab Death." After some minor stage work Theda was chosen to play the lead in the film *A Fool There Was* (1914), and a star was born (or at the very least manufactured). The film was a sensation and the word "vamp" was introduced into the American lexicon. Between 1914 and 1926 she starred in fifty motion pictures, typically as an amoral creature bent on destroying the soul of some poor victim (male, of course), with titles like *The Devil's Daughter*, *Sin*, *Siren of Hell*, *The She Devil*, and *When a Woman Sins*. Theda is pictured here in a very daring costume from the 1917 version of *Cleopatra*. (JC Archives)

SCENE STILL

Typical of the assembly-line features churned out in the 1930s, *Housewife* (First National, 1934) ranks among the worst in the long show business career of Bette Davis (1908–89). In the film, advertising executive George Brent (pictured with a then-blonde Bette in the third of eleven films they made together) leaves his devoted wife and has quite a good time with his vampish ex-girlfriend (Bette), only to learn the error of his ways. Bette played spoiled, headstrong, and self-involved women to perfection, and always rose to the occasion even in inferior productions like this one. Through hard work and perseverance she gradually earned the respect of colleagues and audiences alike, and went on to become one of Hollywood's most durable icons. (JC Archives)

INTERVIEW

The Lady. The Legend. The Legs!

a chat with ANGIE DICKINSON

SCENE STILL

Angie, seen here in a sexy moment with John Cassavetes in *The Killers* (Universal, 1964), took bad girls to a whole new low as the scheming Sheila Farr in this classic film noir based on a short story by Ernest Hemingway. Originally filmed for television but deemed too violent, the film was later released in movie theaters.

HAVING made her mark on the big screen in fifty-six features and the small screen in twenty-five TV movies, two series, three mini-series, and more than two hundred guest spots, Angie Dickinson's status as a show business icon is most definitely secure. Ever since the starlet made her film debut at the age of twenty-three in the Doris Day comedy *Lucky Me* (Warner Bros., 1954), Angie has portrayed some very memorable bad girls, some deliciously naughty and some just downright deadly! So as she celebrated her golden anniversary in the entertainment industry the actress agreed to be interviewed for this book. This author was honored, and Angie was warm, insightful, funny, objective, self-effacing, and clearly comfortable in her position as a Hollywood legend. Here is an excerpt of my chat with North Dakota's most beautiful export conducted on June 8, 2004.

Tony Turtu: Bette Davis once said that she enjoyed playing all those hateful women because ultimately that's what audiences remember. Do you agree?

Angie Dickinson: Not outright, because they also remember Audrey Hepburn in *A Nun's Story*. I would just say that if you can't get a good girl role then get a bad girl role. A good role is great no matter what, but they're likely to remember the bad girls.

TT: As far back as *Tennessee's Partner* [RKO, 1955] you played a saloon girl. Why do you think producers cast you in so many Westerns?

AD: Westerns were very popular at the time, and I did a lot of saloon girls and a lot of Westerns because that was the most common form of entertainment for unskilled actors [*laughs*]. You see I couldn't do Shakespeare, but I could do a saloon girl. Westerns did not require great acting, just presence.

TT: You once said that sometimes Westerns were a thankless job for an actress. Having done so many, do you still feel that way?

After a messy breakup with his pampered mistress (Angie), a sensitive architect (Troy Donahue) finds love with a less complicated American schoolteacher (Suzanne Pleshette) in *Rome Adventure* (Warner Bros., 1962). Angie (at her most ravishing) and the romantic Max Steiner score are the two standouts in this glossy and lavish potboiler also known as *Lovers Must Learn*.

AD: That was a poor choice of words. Let's just say the roles are never very demanding and therefore you can't really strut your stuff. They're quite limited because life was limited then. The Western was the life at that time, which was a simple life, so if you don't have a complicated time, you don't have complicated people. The simpler the story is and the simpler the setting is, naturally less demand is made. *Open Range* would never have been made back in the 1950s because it was quite complex compared to most of the Westerns that were made in the 1950s.

TT: They did seem to have a formula — good guy/bad guy, good girl/bad girl.

AD: Yes, and nothing was better than *Gunsmoke* with that simple formula. [Angie appeared on the classic television Western in 1957 in the episode "Sins of the Father."] But it did not require a great demand for an actor, so it was perfect; it became my schooling. I learned on the job, but I was not doing Dostoyevsky [*laughs*]!

TT: That seemed to change somewhat when *Rio Bravo* (Warner Bros., 1959) came along.

AD: That's one of the unique Westerns. I always said *Destry Rides Again* and *Rio Bravo* have the two best female leads ever in a Western.

TT: Your character, Feathers, moved so easily in what was, at that time, a male-dominated genre. Do you think that's what set it apart and made it so special?

AD: Not only [that but] because Ricky [Nelson] was so cute and special. He was that sidekick that was adorable. Walter Brennan was so funny and cute and Duke [John Wayne] was more warm and lovable, instead of just being a hero; he was also a sexy man, and that also set it apart. Then, of course, you had the camaraderie with Dean Martin, so it was the whole combination. And the suspense. It's really a suspense movie. Are they going to get the guy out before they kill everybody? It's really built on suspense. And it's the great Howard Hawks [the director].

TT: I wanted to ask you about *The Last Challenge* [MGM, 1967], which I've always liked. To me, at least, your character seemed to be more of an asset to the hero [Glenn Ford] than was usually afforded to a female lead.

AD: She was quite assertive. The thing is, that was 1966 and already you were seeing women being more than, as I used to say, "waving goodbye."

TT: You mean, decoration?

AD: Yes, decoration. And so it was a pleasant choice. It was not just bland.

TT: Did you enjoy going back to the Western after so many years and doing *Klondike Fever* [CFI, 1980]?

AD: [*laughs*] You know, *Klondike Fever* is not so bad. It has that awful title.

TT: The title is very 1950s.

AD: [*laughs*] That's true too. But it's not a bad movie at all; it's quite good. Jeff East was in it, but it was fun because it was really quite a classic Western. The girls coming to town to be hookers during the Gold Rush — it was the expected material but it was great fun, especially being up in the Rockies in Canada.

TT: Having those wonderful locations certainly didn't hurt the film.

AD: The experience was wonderful. The experience was more wonderful than the picture, but the picture is not so bad. If they had changed the title I think they might have gotten a little more respect.

TT: We can leave the Westerns for a while. I wanted to ask you about *Ocean's Eleven* [Warner Bros., 1960] and Beatrice Ocean, your character, and how wonderfully she moved through that film, which had a kind of "guys only" feeling.

AD: I was barely in that. I am a slight distraction, and that's about the best you can give it. But you can tell with Danny Ocean [Frank Sinatra] that they were very attracted to one another but he had obviously gambled too much of his life and she wasn't going to take it anymore.

TT: She certainly was strong willed.

SCENE STILL

Cunning and clever Wilma McClatchie (Angie) and her two dangerous daughters (Susan Sennett, third from left, and Robbie Lee, far right) orchestrate a bank-robbing crime spree with the help of two con artists (William Shatner, far left, and Tom Skerritt, second from right) in the Roger Corman-produced cult favorite *Big Bad Mama* (New World Pictures, 1974).

AD: Yeah, it was not easy to shake my head "no" to him. [*laughs*] Boy, I wish they had a sequel that time, 'cause I'd have said "yes" this time! I was very lucky to be in *Ocean's Eleven*, because for the amount of work that's in there — I have dined! [People can] say, "Hey she's in *Ocean's Eleven*." That's nice.

TT: What did you think of the remake? [*Angie has a cameo in the 2001 version.*]

AD: I loved it. It was great fun, and I thought, "What can they do?" and my God, it was wonderfully done. It was really good.

TT: I'd like to talk about *The Killers* [Universal, 1964], which is really an unflinching movie. It's so gritty.

AD: We're all so bad! You talk about bad. That's about as bad as you can get.

TT: The thing that I liked about the film is that there wasn't the usual attempt to redeem everyone. Nobody has an epiphany at the end.

AD: She [Angie's character, Sheila Farr] was turning on him to the end.

TT: Boy, she was really double-dealing!

AD: A double-dealer all the way — as you say, "up to the last minute." I was begging Lee Marvin [she mimics Lee Marvin's line hilariously], "Lady, I don't have the time."

TT: Were you afraid to come across as so unsympathetic? Did it ever give you pause?

AD: No.

TT: It's so good.

AD: It is. The two-timing, the double-crossing! She flipped over and flipped back and flipped over! I think she's the most . . . I don't know what word is. I don't want to say awful . . . perhaps vicious?

LOBBY CARD

A frontier marshal (Glenn Ford, pictured) finds himself targeted by a vicious local thug (Chad Everett) in the colorful Western *The Last Challenge* (MGM, 1967). Angie (seen here trying to help Glenn avoid a deadly showdown) found herself once again in a saloon setting, only this time her character owned the joint.

TT: She is the most duplicitous character. She's a schemer.

AD: Yes, a schemer. She's the worst trashy woman I've ever played. I can't think of one where I'm worse — and doing it with such adoring femininity and all. Of course, she won them over; she was just luscious — from the outside! It is a good movie. That was the first movie made for television.

TT: Was it the very first TV movie?

AD: Yes. There were three made and that was one of them. They made three to show to NBC; before that [films] went to a movie theater, and then [they] went to television. Yeah, that was the first one. NBC said, "We love the idea but not that one." [*laughs*] And so it was just pushed out. It was really a B movie, it was done on a TV budget.

TT: But now it enjoys this cult following.

AD: But at the time you could see why [Ronald] Reagan [her costar] would be embarrassed to be in what was essentially a B movie. It's not in the library, I can guarantee you. [Ronald Reagan, also playing against type, apparently hated the film, which was also his last.]

TT: But it still holds up.

AD: It does. Lee Marvin and [John] Cassavetes are wonderful, and I'm good, so it's worthwhile.

TT: Let me ask you about *Cry Terror* [MGM, 1958] which is another very unsympathetic part.

AD: Fabulous! That was my first real gun moll character. I think it was my first evil, evil character.

TT: She was mean.

AD: Oh, she would have slit that kid's throat! [The kid is costar Jason Mason's kidnapped daughter in the film.] It really gave me a chance to shine, and when I saw it I said, "Hey, I've got something." I then knew that I had it. I knew I was good.

TT: That was your first realization?

AD: Yeah, because it really was good and not "Angie." I was playing a part.

TT: You really lost yourself in a character.

AD: And it was terrific. *Cry Terror* and *The Killers* are the two most evil women that I played and I think they're both wonderful. *Cry Terror* is obvious — she is obviously a killer; but in *The Killers* she is not obviously duplicitous; she's very cunning. And that's nice to have — totally different evil people, but very evil.

TT: I wanted to ask you about *China Gate* [Fox, 1957]. You played Lucky Legs. If you ever write your autobiography, that's the title.

AD: [*laughs*] That's a very interesting point.

TT: Was it fun to make?

AD: I wouldn't call it fun. Sammy Fuller was a wonderful director, but he was tough, and it was a low-budget movie. Low-budget movies are always tough because you have to work so much faster. Of course, it was my first leading role and it was very brave of him to take somebody totally unknown, but I got it and I was good.

TT: While you were doing *Police Woman* [Angie's hit television series; NBC, 1974–1978] you were making, almost simultaneously, *Big Bad Mama* [New World Pictures, 1974].

AD: In that one I wouldn't call me "bad," I would call me "adventurous"! Adventurous and "stops at nothing."

TT: Enterprising?

AD: Oh, God, yes. That's a very funny movie. My daughter and I play it all the time. She loves it.

TT: Did you like doing the sequel, *Big Bad Mama II* [Concorde Pictures, 1987], as well?

AD: I hated it. I was too old for it; I had no energy. That's one I wish I could take back. It's the only movie I wish I hadn't done. But *Big Bad Mama* [the original] was great because she just stopped at nothing and thought it was fine. As she says, "We need it more than they do, honey"!

TT: It's interesting because the film has a lighthearted feel to it, and that works.

AD: It really does. If you could forget *Bonnie and Clyde*, then it would be a very good movie, but it so takes advantage of everything *Bonnie and Clyde* did that it's embarrassing. They even use the same kind of music — the Jew's harp. When the minister falls out of the car, that's what [happened in] *Bonnie and Clyde*! I said, "Can't they be a little more original than that?" So it's embarrassing from that point of view, but, listen, it's a Roger Corman B movie. It's great fun and [William] Shatner is wonderful in it.

PUBLICITY STILL

Angie pulls out the heavy artillery in this still from *China Gate* (Fox, 1957). In this campy action film (with a strong anti-Communist slant), Angie portrayed Lucky Legs, a Eurasion smuggler and saboteur in Vietnam who helps a band of mercenaries blow up an arms depot on the war-locked Chinese border.

TT: And a lot of people would probably not even remember that he did it.

AD: I'm sure not — namely him! [*laughs*] But he's wonderful in it. He's such a con man and when they first meet in the stable, it's one of the best scenes. When you look at it separate from *Bonnie and Clyde*, it's a very nice movie. And to think he's sleeping with all of them. Forget the morality!

TT: It works on an entertainment level, 100 percent.

AD: It does, thank you.

TT: Another movie I wanted to ask you

about is *Charlie Chan and the Curse of the Dragon Queen* [ACI, 1981].

AD: That might be the second one I would take off [my film list]. [Angie played the Dragon Queen in the title.]

TT: Really, because that gave you the opportunity to play a bad girl but you did it with a great deal of humor. It was almost a parody of the bad girls.

AD: I don't know. I have to see it. I saw it, I think, only once and I haven't seen it in so long. When I took the part I wanted to work with Clive Donner [the director] because he had done *What's New Pussycat?* and that was my ex-husband's [music legend Burt Bacharach] breakthrough [in]to the movies. And so I loved *Pussycat* and I wanted to work with Clive. But I went in for hair and makeup and they put on the black wig when I had envisioned myself blonde. [*laughs*] I looked so awful in that black wig that I had no more objectivity. I just simply lost it. So that would be the second one I wish I'd never done.

TT: Interestingly, as opposed to *Big Bad Mama*, it wasn't financially successful so it just seemed to fade away.

AD: I had forgotten it was Michelle Pfeiffer's first movie.

TT: And Peter Ustinov is in it.

AD: And Rachel Roberts and Roddy McDowall — a wonderful cast, but it just didn't add up. Now twenty-four years later I really should look at it and see if it has any worth, but I don't think [it does].

TT: I wanted to ask you about *The Maddening* [Trimark Pictures, 1995]. Now, in that one . . .

AD: Oh, she was simply nuts.

TT: But you always seemed to avoid the horror movie route in your career and I don't believe you ever did it again. Was there any reason that you said, "This isn't for me; one is enough"?

AD: No, by this time I was not getting many offers anyway, and Burt [costar

good, very convincing. That character is very flawed; she seems broken.

AD: You're very observant. She was supposed to be broken.

had to achieve her mission and went about it with great fervor and dedication until she got her man. So I think it's the sincerity. Even in *China Gate*, as young as I was, I was a tough kid in China and a pretty ballsy girl! I think my definition of a good actor is always believability. That is great acting, when you totally believe that [actor] is that person.

" I've played some good 'bad girls' "

Burt Reynolds] is a wonderful friend and he's so loyal. He always has his friends in his movies.

TT: He loves movies.

AD: He gives us all jobs when he can and I think he thought he was doing me a favor. But I was just not very good. I just can't bear to think about it. And also, to tell you the truth, when I read [the script] I thought that movie was a comedy. The director and the producer came to the house to talk about it. I hadn't said yes yet and I said, "You know what would be funny?" I explained a scene, and they just kind of stared at me. I thought, "Oh shit!" [*laughs*] It was so absurd, I thought it was a comedy!

TT: It was very spooky. It reminds me of a film that Tallulah Bankhead made many years before called *Die! Die! My Darling!*

AD: I know the title but I never saw it.

TT: She did to Stephanie Powers what you did to Mia Sara. There were several similarities. I always like horror movies, so I liked *The Maddening*.

AD: I'd have to look at it again and separate myself. You know, you have to try to be objective. But basically I think it's not bad and I thought Danny Huston [the director] did a great job. We used to call it "our little Psycho" on the set. I took it because I adore Burt and any chance to work with him. I thought I'd be good, but I wasn't very good.

TT: I disagree. I think you were very

TT: You've been a major presence in movies and television for such a long time. To what do you attribute your appeal?

AD: The one thing I think I always am, or I have tried to be, is sincere. When you say "a broken woman," I don't even

TT: I'll tell you exactly when that came across to me in a performance of yours. It was a television movie called *The Suicide's Wife* [CBS-TVF, 1979]. That's one of the finest performances you've ever given.

SCENE STILL

A nurse (Angie), implicated in a chocking scandal, lands on the witness stand during the tension-filled courtroom finale of *The Bramble Bush* (Warner Bros., 1960), when a New England doctor (Richard Burton) goes on trial for a mercy killing. Jack Carson (pictured) played a very corrupt lawyer and Angie's shady boyfriend in this sizzling small town soap opera.

realize that, but instinctively I [became] that broken woman. You can't explain that sort of thing.

TT: You did. You lost yourself in that part. She's very sad.

AD: Yes, just like in *The Killers*. She was such a sensuous woman and she

AD: Again I tried to be different. I was trying to shake the *Police Woman* image, because it was right after *Police Woman* and I shook it too far. If I had to do it over again I would never have cut my hair that short and become that different. But there you are, I just tried for sincerity. I've played some good "bad girls"!

CHAPTER ONE

THERE'S A GUN IN MY PURSE

When women go wrong, men go right after them.
—Mae West

HEN Hollywood first decided to explore the seamy underbelly of corruption and organized crime as a theme, the bad girl found a permanent home on the big screen. We were introduced to what we came to know as the doll, the dish, the dame, or — the juiciest moniker of them all — the tomato. If these cynical women weren't covered in mink, you could bet they had a plan on how to get one! During the 1930s and early 1940s these bad girls were still as conscience free as ever, only now our gals paid a hefty moral price for all their indiscretions. This placated the increasingly conservative ticket buyers (and hypocritical studio moguls) who preferred their plot resolutions to be crystal clear; judgments had to be swift and punishments severe. During the classic period of the film noir (roughly between 1940 and 1959) the cinema's bad girls were sadly more pessimistic. They understood the repercussions of their actions, but they followed those paths, however illegal or untoward, in spite of it. These sinners in satin could still be cruel and callous; they could lead a man astray with just a wink and drive him to abandon his wife (or, in some cases, his senses), but goodness — and dare I say virtue — usually won. Happily, the resurgence of the crime drama (some with a distinct retro flavor) in recent years indicates that there is still life (regardless of how cheap) in these silver-screen jezebels. Lena Olin, Linda Fiorentino, Jessica Lange, Anjelica Huston, Annette Bening, and Kathleen Turner are only a few of the actresses who have helped put a fresh spin on a durable genre. Keep on the lookout!

SCENE STILL

The usually more demure (and brunette) Barbara Hale (1921–) played against type as a cool blonde gun moll in *The Houston Story* (Columbia, 1956), costarring Gene Barry (right) as a greedy thug who plans to siphon oil from pipelines and sell it to a crime syndicate. Paul Richards (center) rounded out the cast of this fast-paced caper highlighted by Barbara's saucy performance as a kept woman. (JC Archives)

co-starring JOHN BROMFIELD · MARTHA VICKERS · ROBERT HUTTON and ROSEMARIE BOWE
Produced and Directed by W. LEE WILDER
Screenplay by FRED FREIBERGER · Based on a story by MINDRED LORD
Released thru UNITED ARTISTS

"THE BIG BLUFF"

Robert Hutton confronts his unfaithful wife, a cheap nightclub singer, played by Rosemarie Bowe (1932–) in the gritty crime drama *The Big Bluff* (United Artists, 1955). Rosemarie was a busy young starlet in the 1950s, but she only worked sporadically during her marriage to actor Robert Stack; it was truly one of Hollywood's happiest unions.

A boyishly handsome gun fanatic (John Dall) is seduced into a felonious life by the wanton Peggy Cummins (1925–) in the frank and very intense *Gun Crazy* (King Bros., 1949), which follows the young couple on a brutal cross-country crime spree. The film, originally released as *Deadly Is the Female*, made Peggy a sex symbol and ranks as one of the best couples-on-the-run pictures. Its popularity is due in no small part to Peggy's raw and uninhibited performance, which contributed to its lasting cult fascination. (JC Archives)

"Johnny
Stool Pigeon"

A UNIVERSAL-INTERNATIONAL PICTURE

A convict (Dan Duryea) gets sprung from prison when he agrees to help bring down a gang of heroin smugglers in *Johnny Stool Pigeon* (Universal, 1949), but a troublesome gun moll played by Shelley Winters (1922–) could ruin his plan. Shelley was groomed by the studio to be its resident glamour puss, an image she came to resent and eventually rebel against.

They didn't come any prettier than Yvonne Romain (1938–), a London-born former model who decorated a number of British horror movies in the late 1950s. In *The Frightened City* (Allied Artists, 1961) Yvonne (center) was the mistress of an underworld mastermind (Herbert Lom) who sings at one of his joints. Flanking Yvonne is character actor Neal Arden (left) and starlet Sheena Marshe (right). Yvonne has been married to legendary composer Leslie Bricusse for many years.

Mark Stevens (pictured) directed and costarred with Joan Vohs (1927–2001) in *Cry Vengeance* (Allied Artists, 1951) as a hoodlum seeking revenge on his gangland cronies who sent him up the river. Joan was once again the syndicate floozy in a role she perfected in a string of cheapies in the 1950s. The former Rockette grew tired of the typecasting and moved into light comedy as a semi-regular on the sitcoms *Bachelor Father* and later *Family Affair*.

The gorgeous Constance Smith (1928–2003) helps Bruce Bennett (shown here manhandling his pretty moll) run a racket that scams innocent charities in *The Big Tip Off* (Allied Artists, 1955). Things fall apart when they become the target of a newspaper expose. Constance grew tired of Hollywood and worked in Europe for the remainder of her career, usually playing femme fatales in routine Italian films.

An ex-soldier (Lloyd Bridges) returns to post-war England only to find his former girlfriend played by Moira Lister (1923–) is involved with a gang of racketeers in *The Limping Man* (Lippert, 1953). Born in South Africa, Moira made her film debut in 1943 and usually played spiteful yet sexy society women in some thirty movies.

A Date With Death (Pacific International, 1959), filmed in Psychorama, no less, would barely warrant a footnote in crime-film history if not for the larger-than-life exploits of its star, Liz Renay (1926–), seen here with actor Robert Clarke. Shortly after the release of the film, Liz was subpoenaed to testify against some of the underworld figures she knew from her days as a nightclub showgirl and rising starlet. She refused to turn states evidence, was convicted of purgery, and sentenced to a three-year prison term in 1961. Her subsequent autobiography, *My Face For the World to See*, caused a media sensation and was a worldwide best seller. Liz cemented her cult status by starring in *Desperate Living* for director John Waters in 1977.

Audrey Long (1924–) was a model before she decorated a number of minor pictures. In *Post Office Investigator* (Republic, 1949) the deadly doll makes trouble for the title character (Warren Douglas), who is taken for a ride by Audrey and Tony Gannon. (JC Archives)

21

The icy Lyn Thomas (1929–) makes a convincing argument for never picking up blondes in tight sweaters on desolate roads. Ralph Sanford is the unlucky driver in *Alaska Passage* (Associated Producers, 1959), a film about truck hijackers in the title state. Overall Lyn made nearly fifty films and television appearances, but her workload declined sharply by the early 1960s and she chose to call it quits.

Where would down-at-heel amnesiacs be if they didn't get mixed up with dangerous blondes? *Blackout* (Lippert, 1954) featured Dane Clark as the ill-fated guy involved with a shapely package of trouble played by Belinda Lee (1935–61). Belinda's promising career in British B pictures was cut short when she was killed in a car accident in Italy, where she frequently worked.

22

In *Danger Is My Beat* (Allied Artists, 1955) a hard-boiled blonde, played by Barbara Payton (1927–67), is indicted for murder, but when she sees the man she is charged with killing, Barbara smells a frame-up. Luckily a trusting cop (Paul Langdon) agrees to help her in this taut little B picture. Sadly, this would be Barbara's last film. Years of reckless behavior and alcoholism had taken their toll and left her a much too risky choice for movie producers. Barbara's 1963 autobiography, *I Am Not Ashamed*, is unflinching and brutal in its honesty but failed to lead to any additional work.

Murder along the waterfront was the story in *The Devil's Henchmen* (Columbia, 1949), a harmless programmer featuring Mary Beth Hughes (1919–95) as Silky, a gangland moll, seen here with a young sailor who is about to join her for a nightcap. Most of these parts were strictly routine and didn't allow Mary Beth to use her natural comedic gifts. One highlight, though, was a chance to recreate the role of Kitty Packard in a live television production of *Dinner at Eight* (1955). The character was originally made famous by Jean Harlow in the film version.

LOBBY CARD

(Below) Generations of baby boomers might be surprised to know that this gun-toting dame was also the kindly Mrs. Olsen on the Folgers Coffee commercials for twenty-one years. Actually Virginia Christine (1920–96) appeared in one hundred films and sixty television shows before becoming a much-loved TV spokeswoman. In *The Invisible Wall* (Fox, 1947) a returning GI (Don Castle) gets involved with an icy blonde (Virginia), which leads to a case of mistaken identity and eventually murder. (JC Archives)

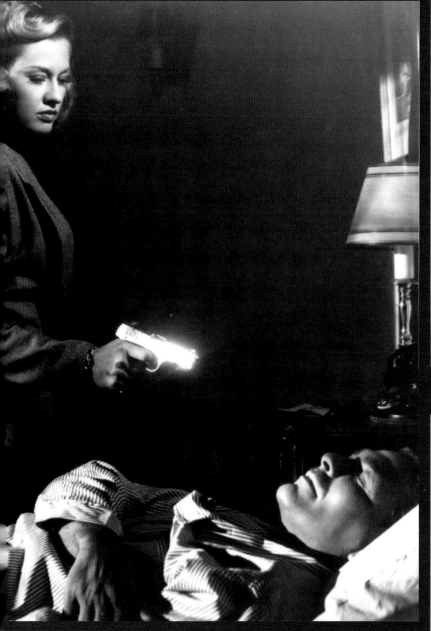

(Above) A smitten reporter (Hugh Beaumont) falls hard for a married woman, played by B movie legend Ann Savage (1921–) in *Apology for Murder* (PRC, 1945), unaware that she plans to knock off her husband. Though heavily derivative of the classic noir *Double Indemnity*, this smaller (but no less gritty) film stands on its own, due in large part to Ann's positively feral performance. (JC Archives)

BENEDICT BOGEAUS presents

SLIGHTLY SCARLET

JOHN PAYNE · ARLENE DAHL · RHONDA FLEMING

James M. Cain's high-voltage drama of a vice-ridden city!

SUPERSCOPE

with
KENT TAYLOR · TED de CORSIA · LANCE FULLER · Directed by ALLAN DWAN · Screenplay by ROBERT BLEES · Produced by BENEDICT BOGEAUS

Print by
TECHNICOLOR

Another James M. Cain novel gets the big, gaudy Hollywood treatment in *Slightly Scarlet* (RKO, 1956), a sordid saga of small town corruption starring Arlene Dahl (1924–) — pictured with perennial movie tough guy Ted de Corsia — as a venal harlot who competes with her only slightly more redeemable sister Rhonda Fleming (1923–) for the love of an honest (or is he?) politician (John Payne).

Ultimate movie queen Joan Crawford (1904–77) supplies some menace to the magazine *Nuit et Jour* (Belgium, June 1947). Amazingly Joan's body of work spanned sΔ33 ix decades and nearly ninety films, so it's hard to believe that by the early 1940s Hollywood declared her "box-office poison" and predicted that her career was over. However, Joan bounced back with a vengeance and won an Oscar to boot for *Mildred Pierce* in 1945, which ushered in a new chapter of aggressive (if a bit more mature) femme fatale roles. For sheer star wattage and a tenacious staying power, Joan had few equals.

Swamp Women (Woolner, 1955) boasted not one but four of the toughest babes ever captured on celluloid. The malevolent quartet (Marie Windsor, Susan Cummings, Carole Matthews, and Beverly Garland) escape from a women's prison to hunt down a cache of buried loot. Here we see Beverly (1926–) dealing with a hostage (Mike Connors) in this ultracheap guilty pleasure. Garland was the Queen of the Bs during the 1950s, but it was on television where she was given more of a chance to stretch as an actress in literally hundreds of guest shots. (JC Archives)

CINÉ REVUE

Veronica LAKE

DANS CE NUMÉRO :
*La Glorieuse
Ascension de*
VERONICA LAKE
par Joan Mac Trevor
★
25ᵉ ANNÉE — Nᵒ 45
9 NOVEMBRE 1945
TOUS LES VENDREDIS
Prix : 7 fr. 50

Cool, aloof beauty Veronica Lake (1919–73) is featured on *Cine Revue* (France, November 1945) at the height of her popularity in the 1940s. Her appearance as a self-destructive floozy in *I Wanted Wings* (1939), put Veronica on the Hollywood fast track, and her bad girl status was secured with three classic film noirs: *This Gun for Hire* (1942), *The Glass Key* (1942), and *The Blue Dahlia* (1946), all costarring Alan Ladd. Their pairing (filled with a palpable sexual tension) was a huge hit with moviegoers, but sadly her peek-a-boo hairstyle (her silky blonde hair seductively falling over one eye — a look that women all over the world copied) garnered more press than her acting ability. Veronica's participation in several second-rate vehicles and her notorious temperamental nature contributed to the demise of a once red-hot career. Aside from a few dreadful films later in the 1940s, Veronica's moment in the sun came to an end.

BARBARA STANWYCK · STERLING HAYDEN

HER HUSBAND WAS LYING SO CLOSE... THE GUN WAS EVEN CLOSER... NOW SHE WAS ONLY ONE SIN AWAY FROM THE

CRIME OF PASSION

The stripped-of-shame story of a cop's wife who committed one sin too many!

A BOB GOLDSTEIN PRODUCTIONS presentation · co-starring **RAYMOND BURR** · with VIRGINIA GREY · FAY WRAY · ROYAL DANO · Story and Screenplay by JOE EISINGER · Executive Producer BOB GOLDSTEIN · Produced by HERMAN COHEN · Directed by GERD OSWALD · Released thru UNITED ARTISTS

Screen legend Barbara Stanwyck (1907–90) contemplates a very sinister deed in *Crime of Passion* (United Artists, 1957) with Sterling Hayden as her less aggressive spouse. This cheaply made crime drama about a domineering shrew who stops at nothing to further her husband's career as a detective was the typical kind of film Barbara made later in her career. It wasn't worthy of her talent but she always rose to the occasion with vibrant, gutsy performances that were her trademark. Barbara was nominated for the Oscar four times for *Stella Dallas* (1937), *Ball of Fire* (1941), *Double Indemnity* (1944), and *Sorry, Wrong Number* (1948), and starred on the Western series *The Big Valley* for four seasons (1965–1969).

Perennial TV favorite Betsy Palmer (1929–) made just a handful of films in the 1950s including the noirish crime drama *The True Story of Lynn Stuart* (Columbia, 1958), which featured her as a housewife who infiltrates a gang by posing as a hardened gun moll. Her involvement lands poor Betsy (pictured here with Barry Atwater) in the slammer as she fights to clear her name amidst some unsavory headlines. More than twenty years later Betsy played the ultimate bad girl as Mrs. Vorhees, a murderous psycho in the original *Friday the 13th*.

Gena Rowlands (1934–), under the direction of her husband John Cassavetes, brings both grit and poignancy to *Gloria* (Columbia, 1980). She plays a jaded mob moll who protects a young boy from a bunch of hit men who wiped out his entire family. Gena's Gloria forms an almost maternal bond with the youngster as they adjust to life on the lam together. Gena received an Oscar nomination (and rightly so) for the film.

Mary Costa (1930–) helps swindle the residents of a small town (with the help of her con-man boyfriend) in *The Big Caper* (United Artists, 1957), a well-made little film noir costarring James Gregory (seen here with the lovely Mary). Her film work was sporadic at best (she provided the voice of Princess Aurora in *Sleeping Beauty*), and she concentrated on her singing, making several appearances on Frances Langford's variety show in 1960.

RORY CALHOUN in "THE BIG CAPER" MARY COSTA · JAMES GREGORY with ROBERT H. HARRIS · COREY ALLEN
Screenplay by MARTIN BERKELEY · Produced by WILLIAM C. THOMAS · HOWARD PINE · Directed by ROBERT STEVENS
A Pine-Thomas Production · Released thru United Artists

In *Destination Murder* (RKO, 1950) a devilish mob moll played by Myrna Dell (1924–) lures an innocent guy into an ill-conceived blackmail plot against her lover, a nightclub owner, which has dire consequences for both of them. Myrna was at her best as these icy seductresses, a role she played to perfection in many second features of the 1940s and 1950s. (JC Archives)

LOBBY CARD

RAW and VIOLENT as the book that sold 3,000,000 sizzling copies!

NEVER LOVE A STRANGER

JOHN DREW BARRYMORE · LITA MILAN · ROBERT BRAY

The rise and fall of a mobster, played by John Drew Barrymore (yes, Drew's dad), is chronicled in *Never Love a Stranger* (Allied Artists, 1958), based on the Harold Robbins best seller. The exotic-looking Lita Milan (1933–) was the racketeer's volatile mistress, a juicy role for the up-and-coming starlet. Surprisingly Lita abandoned her career to marry Ramfis Trujillo, the son of a Dominican Republic dictator who was assasinated in 1961. Soon after, Ramfis was overthrown in a military coup, and he and Lita fled the country to settle in Spain. Ramfis died in an automobile accident in the late 1960s, and Lita remained in Madrid.

32

A small-time jewel thief, played by June Havoc (1916–), tries to keep to the straight and narrow in *Once a Thief* (United Artists, 1950), but her affair with a slick con artist could lead her into deeper trouble. Here June (left) struggles with another tough cookie, played by Marie McDonald (1923–65), in this better-than-average crime drama. June (sister of famous strip-tease artist Gypsy Rose Lee) enjoyed great success in vaudeville beginning at the age of five and carved out a solid career in films and on the stage.

LOBBY CARD

Shelley Winters (1922–) makes a very memorable impression as the infamous Ma Barker in Roger Corman's drive-in fave *Bloody Mama* (A.I.P., 1970). The versatile (and relatively unknown) cast included a young Robert DeNiro as a member of Shelley's murderous clan.

LOBBY CARD

In this career-defining role Lana Turner (1920–98) delivered a knockout performance as a restless waitress in a greasy diner in *The Postman Always Rings Twice* (MGM, 1946), though she bore little resemblance to the character in the 1934 James M. Cain novel. Metro gave this whitewashed version the studio's usual gloss but it still retained an aura of steaminess and intense sexual desire between Lana and costar John Garfield (pictured). (JC Archives)

SCENE STILL

SCENE STILL

In *Criss Cross* (Universal, 1948) trouble never came in such a desirable package as Anna Dundee, played by Yvonne De Carlo (1922–), a newcomer to film noir. Temporarily putting aside her usual harem costumes, Yvonne was cast as Dan Duryea's fickle, double-crossing wife who drags ex-boyfriend Burt Lancaster into a flawed robbery scheme in postwar Los Angeles. (JC Archives)

APPOINTMENT WITH A SHADOW

LOBBY CARD

In *Appointment with a Shadow* (Universal, 1959) a hard-drinking reporter played by George Nader (right) cleans up his act just in time to crack a story that gets him involved with some nefarious characters, including Virginia Field (1917–92), who supplies a little mayhem in mink. Virginia made nearly fifty films beginning in 1934 in her native England and was regularly cast in supporting roles as chic but troublesome women opposite some of the biggest stars of the day.

Jan Sterling (1923–2004) and Chuck Connors get to know each other better in the above-average crime drama *The Human Jungle* (Allied Artists, 1954), with Jan playing a hard-boiled police informant targeted by the syndicate. In films since 1947, Jan never gave a bad performance and enlivened even the most mundane scripts, sometimes displaying a nice flair for comedy. In 1954 she was nominated for an Academy Award for *The High and Mighty*.

LOBBY CARD

Oscar- and Emmy-winning actress Cloris Leachman (1926–) picked up a pistol and became *Crazy Mama* (New World Pictures, 1975), which, despite the exploitative title, was an energetic and wonderfully acted B movie about a trio of dangerous dames — Linda Purl (1955–) played her daughter and Ann Sothern (1909–2001) was her gun-toting mother — who go on a cross-country crime spree in the 1950s. The film was directed by future Academy Award-winner Jonathan Demme.

IN 1957 CHERYL DROVE MOM'S CHEVY ON A HEAVY DATE: GOT KNOCKED UP, KNOCKED OVER A BANK, SMASHED FOUR POLICE CARS AND KIDNAPPED HER STEPFATHER

IT WAS A CRAZY YEAR!

CLORIS LEACHMAN in CRAZY MAMA

A race car driver (Peter Fonda, center) and an auto mechanic (Adam Roarke, far left) team up with a thrill-seeking Susan George (1950–) to knock over a supermarket in *Dirty Mary, Crazy Larry* (Academy Pictures, 1974), one of the best violent car-chase actioners that prolifer-ated drive-ins in the 1970s. Susan carved a nice niche for herself as a rather reckless, promis-cuous young woman who enjoyed a walk on the wild side. Her career hit a few speed bumps in the 1980s when she got a bit too old to play danger-loving Lolitas.

Bobbie Jo was a car hop,
she wanted to be a country singer.

He was a hustler
who dreamed he was Billy The Kid.

For a while they
had something...

...and then...

MARJOE GORTNER

Starring In

Bobbie Jo and the Outlaw

Also Starring

LYNDA CARTER

MARK L. LESTER FILM
n American International Release

JESSE VINT · MERRIE LYNN ROSS and GERRIT GRAHAM as 'Magic Ray'

·Produced by LYNN ROSS and STEVE BRODIE · Written by VERNON ZIMMERMAN
"THOSE CITY LIGHTS" SUNG BY BOBBY BARE | Produced and Directed by MARK L. LESTER
Color by Movielab

 R **RESTRICTED** ⬤
Under 17 Requires Accompanying
Parent or Adult Guardian

CHAPTER TWO

PASSPORT TO TROUBLE

There's no such thing as a hard woman, only soft men.
—Raquel Welch

O N screen, bad girls certainly got around, geographically as well as metaphorically. When they outgrew their neighborhoods (or when the neighborhoods outgrew them) these ladies simply took their act on the road, causing trouble on an international scale. Whether on the lam or on the arm of some financier, their far-flung adventures were usually box-office dynamite. The sight of some sable-clad dame set loose in a South American casino, an African trading post, an Asian opium den, or an Alpine villa proved highly entertaining. Keep in mind that in the days before films were made on location, these sumptuous (or seedy) settings were constructed on studios' back lots, and actresses didn't journey much farther than the intersection at Sunset and Gower. It didn't matter one bit if a picture was filmed in Brussels or Burbank or set in Warsaw or as close as Waikiki; if a story featured a faraway flavor we happily bought low-priced tickets for a two-hour trip aboard a boat, a plane, or a sampan with some of the most beautiful (and dangerous) traveling companions ever to slink past a customs agent. If you're looking for an exciting screen itinerary, I might suggest hopping on *The Shanghai Express* or catching a *Flight to Tangier*. Don't be late for your *Appointment in Majorica*! How about an *Affair in Trinidad* with a certain *Panama Lady* while you try to avoid those sultry *Cuban Rebel Girls* in the oppressive *Jungle Heat* during a *Pacific Blackout*? I promise you, losing your luggage will be the least of your concerns. Enjoy the trip — destination: fun!

New Guinea during WWII is the setting for the prisoner-of-war drama *Seven Women from Hell* (Fox, 1961), which took the girls-in-prison plotline and gave it a tropical flavor. French glamour girl Denise Darcel (1925–), second from the right, headed the cast of hard-as-nails captives0△4 at the mercy of sadistic Japanese guards. The rest of the jailbirds are, from left, Pilar Seurat (1938–2001); Margia Dean (1922–); Yvonne Craig, a few years shy of becoming TV's "Batgirl" (1937–); Sylvia Daneel (1930–); Patricia Owens (1925–2000); and Evadne Baker (1937–95). (JC Archives)

The story for *Come On, Marines!* (Paramount, 1934) must have been written in an alcoholic stupor. The Marines are called in to rescue a group of flashy dolls who are stuck on an undisclosed island. Toby Wing (1915–2001) played one of the girls in this racy (for the time) adventure. (This odd movie includes a cross-dressing scene with the Marines wearing the girls' clothing!) Toby, one of the many Jean Harlow look-alikes who descended upon Hollywood in the 1930s, appeared in more than fifty films. Pictured with her are, from left to right, Fuzzy Knight, Richard Arlen, and Duke York. (JC Archives)

In *The Bribe* (MGM, 1949) a federal agent (Robert Taylor) is hot on the trail of a dealer in black-market aircraft parts (John Hodiak) on a corrupt Central American island, but things get complicated when he falls for the guy's wife, a sultry nightclub singer played by the breathtaking Ava Gardener (1922–90). Ava was groomed by Metro to be the studio's resident sexpot, and she fit the bill beautifully. She later proved herself to be a qualified and extremely fine actress. If the term "screen goddess" was designed to apply to anyone, surely it was Ava Gardener.

LOBBY CARD

ROBERT TAYLOR
AVA GARDNER
CHARLES LAUGHTON
VINCENT PRICE
JOHN HODIAK

The Bribe

An undercover man meets the strangest suspects in his strange business.

The beautiful Mediterranean locale was a definite plus in the otherwise predictable *Captain Blackjack* (Classic Films, 1951), a cheaply made tale of narcotic smugglers on the Riviera. A high point in the film is Agnes Moorehead (1906-1974) as a bitter, manipulative socialite (seen here with British actress Patricia Roc). Agnes brought tremendous skill to each of her more than sixty motion pictures, and was nominated for the Academy Award five times, though she never won. She is probably best remembered for playing Endora on the long-running series *Bewitched* (1967–72).

John Cassavetes was a respected (yet sometimes controversial) filmmaker who made a dubious choice with the cheapie *Affair in Havana* (Allied Artists, 1957). Though the ad copy promised a "torrid story," it was in reality a tired plot, redeemed only by authentic Cuban locations. Sara Shane (1926–) was the provocative wife of a crippled man (Raymond Burr) who has a fling with a down-on-his-luck songwriter (Cassavetes). Sara decorated a few potboilers in the 1950s; she was one of the *Three Bad Sisters* in 1956 and steamed up *Tarzan's Greatest Adventure* in 1959, but her career quickly fizzled.

Gary Cooper y
Tallulah Bankhead
en la película Para-
mount «Entre la es-
pada y la pared»

Over the years there were several attempts to turn revered stage actress Tallulah Bankhead (1902–68) into a major movie vamp but none were terribly successful. *The Devil and the Deep* (Paramount, 1932) was one such effort but audiences were not impressed. One bit of publicity for the film, set in lush locales, was a cover story for *Film Selectos* (Spain, April 1934) featuring Tallulah and her costar Gary Cooper.

A writer (Walter Reed) research-ing secret voodoo rituals in South America gets more than he bar-gained for when he meets the beguiling Venus de Viasa, played by Ziva Rodann (1935–), in the laughable *Macumba Love* (United Artists, 1960). The Israeli-born Ziva turned quite a few men's heads during her all-too-brief film career.

LOBBY CARD

MACUMBA LOVE *Blood-Lust* of the VOODOO QUEEN!

in *FLAMING*
Eastman COLOR
WALTER REED
ZIVA RODANN
William WELLMAN, Jr.
JUNE WILKINSON

Produced and directed by
DOUGLAS FOWLEY
music by SIMONETTI

43

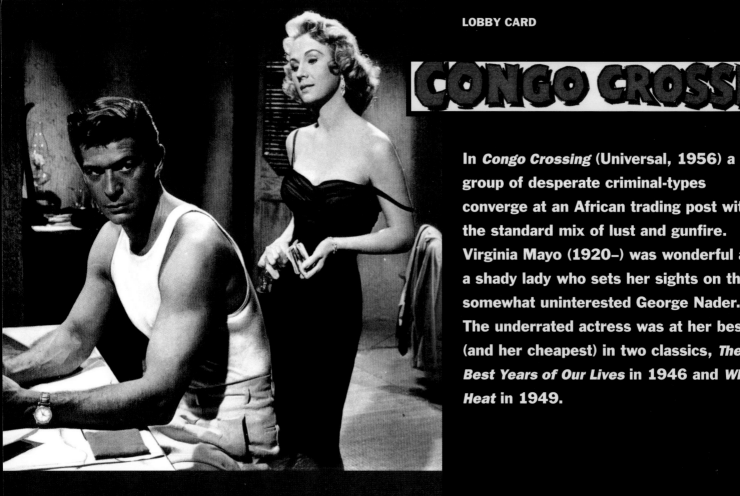

CONGO CROSSING

In *Congo Crossing* (Universal, 1956) a group of desperate criminal-types converge at an African trading post with the standard mix of lust and gunfire. Virginia Mayo (1920–) was wonderful as a shady lady who sets her sights on the somewhat uninterested George Nader. The underrated actress was at her best (and her cheapest) in two classics, *The Best Years of Our Lives* in 1946 and *White Heat* in 1949.

As it happened *The Revolt of Mamie Stover* (Fox, 1956) wasn't much of a revolt after all. When Hollywood decided to turn William Bradford Huie's novel about a prostitute in pre–World War II Hawaii into a film, it was considerably sanitized, to say the least. Jane Russell (1921–) was cast in the title role (only now Mamie is a hostess in a dance hall) and even gets to sing a couple of musical numbers. Still, with Jane in the driver's seat it was a fun ride.

TITLE CARD

SCENE STILL

Riding high on the exploitation bandwagon that dominated the movies in the 1970s was actress Cheri Caffaro (1945–) who, under the direction of her husband Don Schain, appeared in a series of adults-only action films as dynamic CIA operative (not to mention part-time stripper) Ginger MacAllister. In *Girls Are for Loving* (Continental Distributing, 1973) Cheri investigates an insider trading syndicate in an unspecified Asian country (the better not to offend anyone) and is paired (in and out of bed) with an American agent (Timothy Brown). Less sleazy than the other "Ginger" flicks, it nevertheless made a tidy profit thanks to Cheri's devoted following among young male moviegoers (most with fake IDs). (JC Archives)

An investigator (John Archer) is sent to China to ascertain whether one of his company's clients has stolen several million dollars in precious bullion in *Dragon's Gold* (United Artists, 1954). The chief suspect's mysterious wife complicates matters in this nifty low-budget crime drama, which featured Hillary Brooke (1914–99) as yet another conniving dame. With her crisp, perfect diction, Hillary was well suited to play the sophisticated yet predatory other woman in more than eighty films and television shows. It was said that studio-mogul Louis B. Mayer was so impressed with her speaking voice that he signed her to a contract believing she was British!

"DRAGON'S GOLD"   JOHN ARCHER · HILLARY BROOKE

LOBBY CARD

Look

Actress Anna May Wong (1907–61) looks *Dangerous to Know* (Paramount, 1938) on the cover of *Look* (United States, March 1938), especially holding a bloody dagger! Anna May first achieved worldwide stardom as a seductive slave girl in the silent classic *The Thief of Bagdad* (1924) and after many more films she made an easy transition to talkies. Director Josef von Sternberg picked her for *Shanghai Express* (1932), but her subsequent features were low-budget potboilers (*Bombs Over Burma, The Lady From Chungking*, etc.) that profited, rather stereotypically, from Hollywood's love affair with the mysterious Far East and it's aesthetic fascination for all things Asian.

10¢

2,000,000 CIRCULATION

March 1, 1938

World's Most Beautiful Chinese Girl -- SEE PAGE 36

While in England an icy brunette, played by Doris Merrick (1922–) is mixed up with a band of forgery crooks in *The Counterfeiters* (Fox, 1948), and John Sutton (pictured with Doris) helps Scotland Yard put them out of business. Doris worked nonstop for more than a decade and retired shortly after *Untamed Women* (1952) in which she ruled a tribe of lusty, Druid-worshipping jungle girls. (No one could blame her.)

LOBBY CARD

HALF SHEET POSTER

A NEW DIMENSION IN CRIME ...SEX!

"RIFF RAFF GIRLS"

(FORMERLY TITLED "RIFIFI FOR GIRLS")

Their charms were as deadly as their guns... and they knew how to use BOTH!

In spite of the sensational title and poster art (for the American markets), *Riff Raff Girls* (Continental Distributing, 1962) is an exciting crime drama starring international movie siren Nadja Tiller (1949–) as a Brussels nightclub owner determined to succeed at any cost in a ruthless, male-dominated business. *Riff Raff Girls* was one of more than ninety films made by the still-active star.

A millionaire (Omar Sharif) and his mistress, played by Karen Black (1942–), have plans for her wealthy husband, but he in turn has a few tricks of his own for his cheating wife in *Crime and Passion* (A.I.P., 1976). Set in the beautiful Austrian Alps, the film features Karen (seen here with Joseph Bottoms) at her sexiest in one of the more than one hundred features she has made. Oscar nominated for *Five Easy Pieces* and *Easy Rider*, her screen time in recent years has been largely restricted to very, very low-budget productions.

TROY
DONAHUE
ANDREA
DROMM
That "Russians Are Coming" Gal

"COME SPY WITH ME"

ALSO STARRING ALBERT DEKKER · WITH MART HULSWIT · VALERIE ALLEN · WRITTEN BY CHERNEY BERG · BASED ON AN ORIGINAL STORY BY STUART JAMES · EXECUTIVE PRODUCER ALAN V. ISELIN · PRODUCED BY PAUL M. HELLER · DIRECTED BY MARSHALL STONE · COLOR BY DELUXE
An MPO Production in Association with Futurama Entertainment Corporation · Released by 20th Century-Fox

HEAR THE MIRACLES SING — "SPY WITH ME"

48

In *Come Spy With Me* (Fox, 1967) former teen idol Troy Donahue gets more than he bargained for when he helps a beautiful secret agent, played by Andrea Dromm (1941–), as she investigates several killings in the Caribbean. Much hype surrounded Andrea's debut in *The Russians Are Coming! The Russians Are Coming!* the year before, but she failed to establish a foothold in films and vanished from the scene.

Once again the stalwart hero, Robert Hutton is lured into a dangerous situation by a treacherous siren. This time it's the slinky Lisa Gastoni (1935–) in *Thunder Over Tangier* (Republic, 1957), a movie about an international forgery ring. Lisa worked steadily for twenty-five years without slowing down to catch her breath. She starred in some seventy films (in her native Italy and all over the world), including some with torrid titles such as *Female Fiends* and *Callgirls 66*!

THUNDER OVER TANGIER

A SUNSET PALISADES PRODUCTION

PRESS BOOK DETAIL

The Amazonian Tamara Dobson (1947–) is back in action as the title character in *Cleopatra Jones and the Casino of Gold* (Warner Bros., 1975). This time she targets a drug syndicate in Hong Kong run by villainess Stella Stevens (1936–) as the Dragon Lady. Both stars pull no punches as deadly adversaries and they help the film rise above the standard exploitation silliness that flooded the market in the 1970s.

6 ft. 2in. of dynamite caught in the web of international intrigue.

CLEOPATRA JONES AND THE CASINO OF GOLD

TAMARA DOBSON · STELLA STEVENS IN CLEOPATRA JONES AND THE CASINO OF GOLD   A RUN RUN SHAW / WILLIAM TENNANT PRODUCTION   R RESTRICTED Under 17 requires accompanying Parent or Adult Guardian

Written and Produced by WILLIAM TENNANT   Based on characters created by MAX JULIEN   Directed by CHUCK BAIL   TECHNICOLOR® PANAVISION®   from Warner Bros   W   A Warner Communications Company

Estelita (1928–66), who was occasionally billed as Estelita Rodriguez, started appearing in Hollywood films in the mid-1940s, typically as a fiery Latina in low-budget Westerns. There was talk at one time that Estelita might star in a biography of actress Lupe Velez but nothing came of it. She continued to play stereo-typical hellcat roles in nonsense like *Tropical Heat Wave* (Republic, 1952), with Robert Hutton as the object of her affection.

In *Moment to Moment* (Universal, 1965) Jean Seberg (1938–79) is a wealthy businessman's wife who has an affair while living on the Riviera and may be responsible for her lover's murder. Handsome Sean Garrison plays the boyfriend in this glossy mystery. Jean started working in Europe almost exclusively around this time, but the obscure (and often dreadful) films she made there weren't worthy of her talent.

It's been said that 1939 was a banner year for Hollywood, with great successes (*The Wizard of Oz, Dark Victory, Wuthering Heights, Gone with the Wind*, et al) from top studios. Most certainly *Lady of the Tropics* (MGM, 1939) wasn't one of them. Set somewhere in the Malaysian jungle, the critical and commercial flop starred Robert Taylor as a rich playboy and Hedy Lamarr (1913–2003) as a gorgeous half-caste who brings torment to all men, not to mention the audience! This glossy silliness was typical of the kind of films the Austrian-born beauty was featured in during her tenure in Hollywood.

No expense was spared in making the opulent, though dated, *Mata Hari* (MGM, 1932) with Greta Garbo (1905–90) in the title role of the infamous WWI German spy. Garbo was at her most seductive, and the film, even with the historical inaccuracies, was one of her more profitable releases. In this scene she shares an intimate moment with a Russian officer (Ramon Novarro), who will no doubt succumb to her charms.

In *The Happy Thieves* (United Artists, 1962) Rita Hayworth (1918–87) learns that she's been duped by her debonair boyfriend from his nemesis (Gregoire Aslan) in this zany caper about a plot to rob an art museum. Rita, who also coproduced the movie, had a flair for comedy, but the film was ultimately unsuccessful at the box office.

Amidst a backdrop of political turmoil, a prostitute, played by Corinne Calvet (1925–2001), tries to seduce a monk (Charles Boyer) in order to secure a visa that would allow her to leave India in *Thunder in the East* (Paramount, 1952). Corinne portrayed a number of colorful leads in the 1950s, usually as a fallen woman, but her career never really took off despite a huge publicity buildup.

Anthony Quinn takes a much needed break from deep-sea treasure hunting in *City Beneath the Sea* (Universal, 1953), which features starlet Suzan Ball (1933–55) in another exotic part as an entertainer at a tropic café. This role was nothing new for Suzan (Lucille Ball's second cousin), who debuted as a harem girl in *Aladdin and His Lamp* only a year before. Cancer claimed her life shortly after the release of her final film, *Chief Crazy Horse* in 1955. Suzan was just twenty-two.

LOBBY CARD

Constance Dowling (1920–69) began her movie career with a great deal of fanfare when she became a decorative addition to Danny Kaye's lavish debut in *Up in Arms* in 1944. Failing to be cast as anything more than window dressing, Constance left Hollywood by the late 1940s and settled in Rome, where she was eagerly welcomed to the burgeoning film industry there. Here we see Constance at her icy best in the chilling and very atmospheric *Stormbound* (Republic, 1951), a film about lust and infidelity at a rustic cabin. The picture was also released as *The Road Ends at the River*. (JC Archives)

Doris Dowling (1923–2004) had an interesting start in show business with meatier roles in both *The Blue Dahlia* (1946) and *Lost Weekend* (1947) but they sadly didn't lead to anything more substantial. She joined her older sister, Constance, in Italy, where they both enjoyed a long run playing fallen women. In *Bitter Rice* (Lux Film, 1949) Doris plays a petty criminal who seeks refuge among Italian field workers. In this scene she has involved costar Raf Vallone in a robbery and murder plot that doesn't seem to be going too well for either of them. (JC Archives)

Hard-as-nails dish Ruth Roman (1922–99) relieves prospector Gary Cooper of some of his loot in *Blowing Wild* (Warner Bros., 1953), a saga of greed and infidelity on a Mexican oil rig. In her prime Ruth could play cold-hearted opportunists quite convincingly and made an easy transition to character parts in a career that spanned fifty years.

Cyd Charisse (1921–) hung up her dancing shoes temporarily to play a movie producer's (Kirk Douglas) vicious, neurotic ex-wife, who makes his life on an Italian movie set simply unbearable in *Two Weeks in Another Town* (MGM, 1962). Here Kirk has had enough of the shrewish Cyd and threatens to drive their car over a cliff after leaving a party at a hilltop villa.

QUEEN OF THE VILE

Evil is obvious only in retrospect.
—Gloria Steinem

OR years high-camp enthusiasts have extolled the pleasures of watching gladiator epics, south sea island adventures, and other costume spectaculars. The odd appeal must certainly have to do with the occasionally wooden acting, the laughable plotlines, and the typically non-existent production values. Hollywood, in its infancy, knew the value of this escapist fare as far back as 1913 when Helen Gardner became *A Princess of Bagdad*. She was followed by dozens of her silent sisters who undulated in front of painted papier-mâché idols to the delight of an enthralled public. Another highlight had to be the opportunity to catch some of the most glamorous stars of the day trying to navigate their way through these absurd stories. At one time or another Lana Turner, Susan Hayward, Paulette Goddard, and even Lucille Ball had to bow to the demands of studio zexecutives (not famous for their well-developed tastes) and slip on a pair of harem pants for an outing in old Babylon. Other actresses such as Yvonne De Carlo, Maria Montez, and Maureen O'Hara seemed quite comfortable atop a camel or at the bow of a pirate ship, and they brought a wonderful energy to the screen. Make no mistake: these movies could be highly entertaining (if you ignored the sometimes blatant historical inaccuracies) and they almost always made a tidy profit. The chance to view a scantily clad native girl was most appreciated by the largely male audiences, a fact not lost on the producers of this hokum. Featuring big and not-so-big names, these films were churned out at a feverish pace. Devotees of this drivel (rich with evil jungle queens, lusty lady bandits, and assorted panther women) remain eternally grateful.

RHONDA FLEMING RICARDO MONTALBAN in

The Queen of Babylon

Released by 20th CENTURY-FOX *in* Technicolor

In ancient Babylonia, a beautiful shepherdess, played by Rhonda Fleming (1923–), becomes a fabled courtesan in an effort to dethrone an evil tyrant in the Italian quickie *The Queen of Babylon* (Fox, 1956). Roldano Lupi, shown here with the luscious Rhonda, played the dastardly despot. Rhonda was perfectly suited for these escapist adventure yarns and always looked ravishing in harem attire.

LOBBY CARD

Paulette Goddard (1910–90) was nearly forty when she accepted the lead in *Bride of Vengeance* (Paramount, 1949), playing a young Lucretia Borgia. The ill-conceived historical hodgepodge costars (from left to right) Nicholas Joy, Ed Millard, and John Lund. Paulette was one of filmdom's most vivacious stars, but *Bride of Vengeance* proved to be a costly flop and marked the end of a ten-year collaboration between Goddard and Paramount Pictures. **(JC Archives)**

SCENE STILL

The Mongols (Colorama Features, 1961) starred Anita Ekberg (1931–) as Hulina, a lusty barbarian princess, and Jack Palance as the son of Ghenghis Khan and her partner in pillaging. This was just one of the dozens of European films that the Swedish-born bombshell made during the 1960s, when she reigned as an international sex symbol.

The wicked Queen Omphale, played by Sylvia Lopez (1931–59) clutches the muscular thigh (a bad girl move if ever there was one) of Hercules (Steve Reeves) in *Hercules Unchained* (Warner Bros., 1959), one of the better sword and sandal epics. The French-born Sylvia (some sources claim she was Austrian) was discovered modeling for couturier Jacques Fath in Paris, and quickly found herself in demand as decoration (albeit evil) in Italian adventure movies. She was filming *Come Dance with Me* in 1959 with Brigitte Bardot when she discovered she had leukemia. Sylvia never finished the picture (starlet Dawn Addams replaced her), and she died later that year.

The always glamorous Lana Turner (1920–98) was hilariously miscast as a pagan priestess (shown here with Louis Calhern as the evil high priest of the temple) who corrupts all men in *The Prodigal* (MGM, 1955). Even Metro's rather glossy production values couldn't save this clinker, though Lana gave it all she had, including a memorable high dive into a pit of fire at the movie's end.

Joan Shawlee (1926–87) was usually cast as loud, brassy broads, most famously as Sweet Sue, the leader of an all-girl orchestra in the classic comedy *Some Like It Hot*. However, in the ludicrous *Prehistoric Women* (Eagle Lion Films, 1950) Joan (center) traded her baton for a club as a fierce, man-hating cave girl. Here Joan is flanked by two other fur-clad feminists, Kerry Vaughn (1925–, left) and Judy Landon (1930–, right), who both look more Minsky's than Mesozoic! (JC Archives)

She lives by the code of the *Vendetta!*

LOVE is wild...
LIFE is violent...
DEATH is cheap!

HOWARD HUGHES'
production
Vendetta
starring FAITH DOMERGUE

and introducing GEORGE DOLENZ with HILLARY BROOKE · NIGEL BRUCE · JOSEPH CALLEIA
HUGO HAAS · DONALD BUKA · Directed by MEL FERRER · Screenplay by W. R. BURNETT

RKO RADIO

A Howard Hughes discovery, Faith Domergue (1925–99) was a darkly dangerous beauty who starred in *Vendetta* (RKO, 1950), an expensive, top-heavy costume melodrama that went through four (!) different directors (including Hughes himself) before its release. The movie was a dud and Faith's once-promising career slipped into the B ranks by the mid-1950s with roles in undistinguished films around the globe.

PORTRAIT CARD

British actor Richard Greene tries to get up close and personal with the beautiful and feisty daughter of a famous outlaw, played with great zeal by Barbara Hale (1921–) in *Lorna Doone* (Columbia, 1951). Barbara looked quite fetching in seventeenth century costumes. Years later she would take on the role of Della Street, the extraordinary gal Friday on the long-running television series *Perry Mason* (1957–66), for which she is best remembered.

Swashbuckling adventure at its best, this time on the distaff side, with the knockout Gianna Maria Canale (1927–) as *The Queen of the Pirates* (Columbia, 1960). Gianna was one of Italy's most popular stars, and she was especially at home in these spirited adventure tales which, though filmed on modest budgets, were always profitable, specifically with the Saturday-matinee crowds. Two years later Gianna (again with sword in hand) starred in the sequel as *The Tiger of the Seven Seas*.

Action and passion are on deck in *Botany Bay* (Paramount, 1953), an entertaining swashbuckler that centers around a convict ship bound for Australia in the 1790s. James Mason (right) portrayed the ship's captain and Patricia Medina (1921–) was one of the prisoners, albeit a pretty one. Patricia made many of these seafaring adventure yarns during her career and became one of that genre's favorite leading ladies.

DESERT INTRIGUE... DEVILTRY... and EXCITEMENT!

...and the girl whose beauty wove them into a great adventure...with her kisses and caresses!

FORT ALGIERS

YVETTE
A clever beauty in a world of lonely men!

KALAMI
Lusty, gusty, hard-living soldier of fortune!

AMIR
Desert Sheik—leader of fierce Arab hordes!

JEFF
His past was as secret as his deadly mission!

starring

YVONNE De CARLO · CARLOS THOMPSON

with Raymond Burr · Leif Erickson · Anthony Caruso · John Dehner · Sandra Gale · Bill Phipps · Produced by JOSEPH N. ERMOLIEFF

Directed by LESLEY SELANDER · Screenplay by THEODORE ST. JOHN · Associate Producer EDWARD L. ALPERSON, Jr. · Released Thru United Artists

More derring-do in the desert with Yvonne De Carlo (1922–) as a calculating stunner who causes a tribal war (presumably because she's either too calculating or too stunning) in *Fort Algiers* (United Artists, 1953). Yvonne was perfectly comfortable in Westerns and Easterns, as these sandstorm sagas were termed, and she shifted between the two regularly in the 1950s when she was hailed as one of Tinseltown's great beauties.

Acquanetta (1921–2004) was nicknamed the "Venezuelan Volcano" by studio publicists, though there was no proof that she was actually born in Venezuela. She did, however, steam up movie screens in the 1940s in a series of lush jungle adventures and low-budget horror films. Here, as the wicked high priestess Lea, Acquanetta commands a band of crazed tribal cultists in *Tarzan* and the *Leopard Woman* (RKO, 1946), one of Johnny Weissmuller's last outings as the title hero. (JC Archives)

LOBBY CARD

When Ursula Andress (1936–) emerged from the ocean in *Dr. No* (1962) wearing that famous white bikini, the Swiss-born actress created an indelible cinematic moment. Her beauty was staggering and was displayed to its best advantage in more than fifty films, including *She* (MGM/Seven Arts, 1965), with Ursula as an ancient queen of a lost civilization who possesses the eternal flame of everlasting life. John Richardson is the explorer who seeks this magic fire, and lucky for him that he resembles Ursula's long-dead lover. It's convoluted but satisfying fun with nice production values, though the original 1935 version gets most of the critical praise.

Three years before Tina Louise (1934–) set sail for a three-hour tour on the popular sitcom *Gilligan's Island* (1964–67), she played whistle-worthy temptresses in several Westerns and lively costumers like the Italian *Siege of Syracuse* (Paramount, 1961) with Rossano Brazzi. That same year Tina went the Mata Hari-route for *Armored Command*, and was the beautiful Sappho in *Warrior Empress*, a somewhat whitewashed account of the life of the seventh century Greek poetess. More recently Tina turned in several wonderful performances in some interesting independent films, such as *Johnny Suede*, starring a young Brad Pitt.

An explorer discovers a lost civilization of Amazon warriors (where blondes are subservient to brunettes) in *Prehistoric Women* (Hammer, 1967), not to be confused with the 1950 classic of the same name. Here we see the ferocious ruler, played by Martine Beswick (1941–), trying to entice her prisoner (Michael Latimer) with a groovy tribal dance, but he prefers her fairer handmaiden. That's going to cost him! Incidentally, the beauteous Martine has the distinction of being the only actress to appear in three Bond films (*Dr. No, From Russia with Love,* and *Thunderball*) which has solidified her cult status globally.

British actress Patricia Laffan (1919–) served up an ample portion of wickedness — Roman-style — as Poppaea, Nero's scheming mistress, in the top-heavy spectacle *Quo Vadis* (Cinecitta/MGM, 1951). This evil courtesan has been played by everyone from Claudette Colbert to Brigitte Bardot, and Patricia certainly holds her own, even in that lofty company. Here Poppaea looks on as Petronius (Leo Genn) and the emperor (Peter Ustinov) discover more ways to persecute those pesky Christians.

Paulette Goddard (1910–90) was a major film star whose professional fortunes had changed dramatically for the worse when she agreed to make the ludicrous *Sins of Jezebel* (Lippert, 1953) a sub-B picture completed in only four days (surely some kind of record even for B pictures!). As the notorious pagan princess of ancient Jezreel, Paulette seduces the royal Captain of the Guards (George Nader, left) on the very day she is to marry King Ahab of Israel. Naturally this causes repercussions of biblical proportions for all the folks in her orbit. Definitely a career low point for the gorgeous Goddard. (JC Archives)

They don't get more eye-popping than the ultracampy *Song of Scheherazade* (Universal, 1947), one of the first starring roles for Yvonne De Carlo (1922–) who was being groomed as a threat to the studio's temperamental Queen of Technicolor, Maria Montez. Yvonne played Cara de Talavera, the daughter of a Spanish nobleman, who secretly dances at a Moroccan cabaret. It's there that Cara becomes the musical inspiration for a Russian sailor (played by Jean Pierre Aumont), who, as it turns out, is the composer Rimsky-Korsakov! Despite the highly fictionalized plot the film is great silly fun.

Maria Montez (1920–51) was the queen of escapist technicolor action movies during the 1940s and was popular with a war-weary public that didn't want to think too much at their local theaters. Maria supplied the needed juice to these ridiculous camel operas and almost single-handedly controlled the genre. She played good princesses (*Arabian Nights*); bad princesses (*Siren of Atlantis*); and both parts (a dual role in the camp masterpiece *Cobra Woman*). Here we see her in *White Savage* (Universal, 1943), as Tahia, a tropical bad girl and a woman who could ravage the souls of men, at least according to the poster tagline. Maria died of a massive heart attack while taking a saline bath, and her fanatical cult following (largely among gay men) hasn't diminished to this day.

Superior production values highlighted *Anne of the Indies* (Fox, 1951), a colorful seafaring yarn starring Jean Peters (1926–2000) as a lusty lady buccaneer, and Louis Jourdan, who is about to find out exactly who is in charge. Jean played assorted spitfires in several 1950s productions but gave up her promising career to marry reclusive billionaire Howard Hughes. They divorced in 1971 and Jean briefly returned to acting. (JC Archives)

Ursula Andress wasn't available for the sequel to *She*, so Czech starlet Olinka Berova (1943–) filled her toga (and beautifully too) for the inferior *Vengeance of She* (Hammer, 1968) as a mysterious young lady possessed by the spirit of Ayesha, the long-dead queen of the lost kingdom of Kuma. John Richardson (who was in the original) returned as a high priest who reminds the buxom Olinka of her sacred birthright as their eternal ruler. Olinka made some twenty films, most of which were second-rate European thrillers that barely caused a ripple.

Once again Hollywood turned to the Bible for bad girl inspiration, and *Salome* (Columbia, 1953) was the dubious result. Rita Hayworth (1918–87) tried in vain to breathe some life into the story of the *Siren of Galilee* and her famous dance of the seven veils, but despite all the hype the film was a failure. Stewart Granger (pictured with Rita) played the Roman Commander Claudius, who obviously likes what he sees. (JC Archives)

LET THE GAMES BEGIN!
NAKED WARRIORS

Starring PAM GRIER • MARGARET MARKOV • Produced by MARK DAMON
Directed by STEVE CARVER • Written by JOHN & JOYCE CORRINGTON
A Concorde Picture

MGM/UA HOME VIDEO

Concorde

Distributed by MGM/UA Home Video, Inc.
Design © 1988 MGM/UA Home Video, Inc.
All Rights Reserved.

P-204C

Confident, self-assured cult icon Pam Grier (1950–) has been a star for more than thirty years. She rose to fame in a series of ultra-low-budget exploitation films in the 1970s that were gold mines at the box office and possessed a revolutionary pro-feminist viewpoint, something rarely seen in the misogynistic soft-core industry. *Naked Warriors* — originally titled *The Arena* (Concorde, 1973) — was one such ambitious effort starring Pam and Margaret Markov (1951–) as a couple of brutal female gladiators in ancient Rome. In recent years Pam has developed into a fine, competent actress and has kept her substantial sex appeal intact.

The luscious Linda Christian (1924–) starred in *Slaves of Babylon* (Columbia, 1953), a silly Biblical folderol in which she played the alluring Princess Panthea (*grrr!*). Her onscreen roles were never as fascinating as her offscreen life — two marriages to actors Tyrone Power and Edmund Purdom — and played out in gossip columns and jet-set watering holes around the world.) Dubbed the "copper girl" because of her exotic complexion, Linda played other bad girl roles (including *Thunderstorm*, 1956, and *The Devil's Hand*, 1962), in a film career that was sporadic at best.

PUBLICITY STILL

73

Dale Robertson (left) supplied the needed enthusiasm to the title role of *Son of Sinbad* (RKO, 1955), a gaudy Arabian Nights tale featuring future "Fright King" Vincent Price (right) as his comic sidekick and the curvaceous Mari Blanchard (1927–70, center) as a beguiling harem hottie who desires the handsome hero. Mari was quite comfortable in these costume folderols and made several during her career. Blink and you'll miss Kim Novak in an early bit as a lady warrior. (JC Archives)

Legendary Mexican movie siren Maria Felix (1914–2002) journeyed to Italy to play Rome's historically wicked empress in *The Affairs of Messalina* (Columbia, 1953), a daring spectacle with an international cast. Maria, one of Latin America's biggest film stars, declined every Hollywood offer she received over the years, refusing to play the stereotypical hot-blooded peasant girls that the majority of Spanish-speaking actresses were reduced to portraying.

ONE SHEET POSTER

The fabulous adventures of the world's greatest adventuress!

The life of that famous and unscrupulous purveyor of poison becomes the subject of the luridly titled *Nights of Lucretia Borgia* (Columbia, 1960). British starlet Belinda Lee (1935–61) is sufficiently seductive and treacherous (historical inaccuracies aside) as the darling of the Renaissance in one of the several Italian daggers-and-décolletage films she made in her all-too-brief career.

HALF SHEET POSTER

SCENE STILL

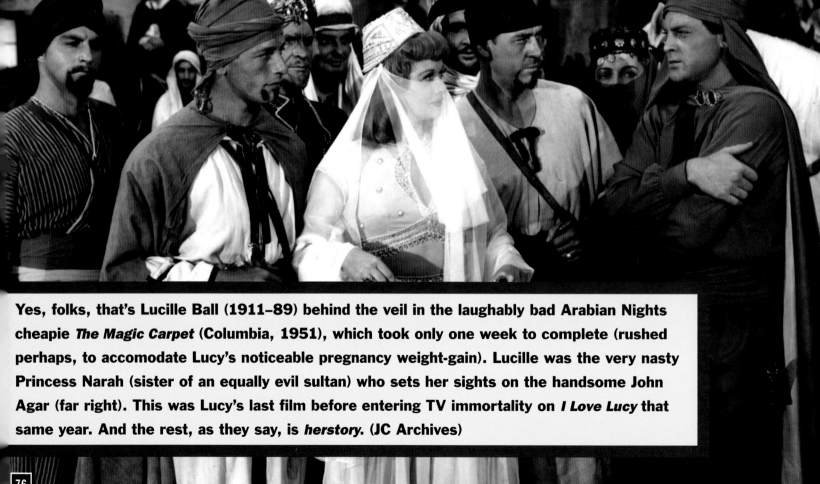

Yes, folks, that's Lucille Ball (1911–89) behind the veil in the laughably bad Arabian Nights cheapie *The Magic Carpet* (Columbia, 1951), which took only one week to complete (rushed perhaps, to accomodate Lucy's noticeable pregnancy weight-gain). Lucille was the very nasty Princess Narah (sister of an equally evil sultan) who sets her sights on the handsome John Agar (far right). This was Lucy's last film before entering TV immortality on *I Love Lucy* that same year. And the rest, as they say, is *herstory*. (JC Archives)

Lady Godiva

PRINT BY *Technicolor*

LOBBY CARD

England's most notorious horseback rider, *Lady Godiva* (Universal, 1955), was the subject of a considerably whitewashed biopic (don't bother straining your eyes — you won't see anything) starring Maureen O'Hara (1920–) as the uninhibited noblewoman. Maureen, seen here with costars (from left to right) Eduard Franz, Victor McLaglen, and George Nader, was certainly no stranger to these costumed adventures and was right at home with sword in hand during her many years as a top leading lady.

The radiant Margaret Lockwood (1916–90) was cast as some of the meanest, most disreputable women in a string of British costumers in the 1940s at the height of her popularity as a major film star. As *The Wicked Lady* (Gainsborough, 1945) Margaret was a lusty lady outlaw terrorizing the English countryside with her accomplice/lover played by James Mason in this robust tale. Faye Dunaway stepped into the gauntlet gloves and boots for the 1983 remake, but Margaret's version is far superior.

A rebellious royal, played by Paula Corday (1920–92), becomes a masked avenger by night in *The Sword of Monte Cristo* (Fox, 1951), as she searches for the title character's hidden treasure. The Swiss-born starlet (who initially billed herself as Rita Corday) played assorted dangerous young ladies (the first at RKO in the 1940s), but her career never really caught fire and she was off the screen by 1956.

More back-lot jungle histrionics, this time with Gale Sherwood (1929–) as the *Blonde Savage* (Eagle Lion Films, 1947), a primitive beauty who rules a mysterious native tribe. In this scene Gale (as the dagger-wielding Meelah) clashes with the faithless wife of a diamond mine owner, played by Veda Ann Borg (1915–73), over Leif Erickson (left). Gale's movie career was a short one, but Veda Ann's went on for years with more than one hundred films to her credit, mostly in second features. (JC Archives)

Once called "The World's Greatest Female Action Star," Sybil Danning (1949–) enjoys a devoted following on both sides of the Atlantic. After a stint in several German soft-core porn films, the Vienna-born stunner made the jump to more mainstream fare and later ruled the direct-to-video adventure market for years, usually as sadistic, sexually insatiable predators. Here Sybil is a Roman swordswoman in ancient Pompeii in the sex-filled (and factually slim) *Warrior Queen* (Lightning Pictures, 1986).

CHAPTER FOUR

LOVELY BUT LETHAL

Eventually, we all play bitches, or we don't work.
—Bette Davis

HEY could be haughty, high-strung, selfish, devious, and delinquent. Of course this is but the tip of the iceberg (or should I say ice queen) in describing the very best of the upper-crust bad girls and her lower-crust girlfriends. They became the kind of characters that movie buffs just love to hate. Was it the way they sipped a cocktail or arched an eyebrow? It's hard to say. We do know that they supplied the oxygen to countless films, irrespective of the budget. Whether they were rage-filled teenagers starved for kicks or man-hungry divorcees craving affection, Hollywood didn't know any socioeconomic limits when it came to the lovely but lethal. The surroundings could be lavish or low rent; the wardrobe denim or Dior. From Gail Patrick in the 1930s to Neve Campbell in the 1990s these devious little darlings always had enough wherewithal to steal another woman's husband (or at least his car) without so much as a backward glance. Alas, the unfortunate bloke usually returned to his long-suffering wife and these savvy troublemakers learned a costly lesson, which almost always involved some kind of public humiliation. This was designed to satisfy all the prudes with the she-got-what-she-asked-for attitudes.

As we watched these silly plots unfold from a comfortable distance (and with these women it was better to have a buffer zone), didn't we hope (for a second or two) that these bad girls might get safely out of town before their dirty deeds were discovered? Naturally the majority of them didn't make it. (Darn that pesky celluloid retribution again!)

An irate father (Don Shelton) resorts to corporal punishment in *High School Hellcats* (A.I.P., 1958) when his daughter, played by Yvonne Lime (1938–), falls in with the wrong crowd. This cautionary tale (with plenty of unintentional bellylaughs) features Yvonne defying the school administrators by wearing blue jeans to class and necking with an older boy from an unacceptable family. Shocking! Yvonne was no stranger to these juvenile delinquent movies but was already too old to be playing troubled teenagers, which is probably why it was so much fun to watch.

...what must a good girl say to "belong"?

THE *FACTS* ABOUT THE TABOO SORORITIES THAT GIVE THEM WHAT THEY WANT!

HIGH SCHOOL HELLCATS

Starring YVONNE LIME · BRET HALSEY · JANA LUND

Produced by CHARLES BUDDY ROGERS · Directed by EDWARD BERNDS · Story and Screenplay by MARK and JAN LOWEL · A JAMES H. NICHOLSON and SAMUEL Z. ARKOFF Production · An AMERICAN-INTERNATIONAL Picture

Marla English (1930–), a bargain-basement Liz Taylor, is one of *Three Bad Sisters* (United Artists, 1956), a tawdry tale about the nasty titular trio who fight tooth and nail over their late father's inheritance. Handsome John Bromfield (pictured with Marla) has the misfortune of tangling with these murderous mantraps in this guilty pleasure. Much to the disappointment of her many fans, Marla made just a handful of films before calling it quits.

Another entry from the it's-so-bad-it's-good category, *Where Love Has Gone* (Embassy, 1964) offered the vivacious Joey Heatherton (1944–) as a spoiled teenager who is packed off to a reform school after being accused of murdering her mother's lover. Mike ("Mannix") Connors played her sympathetic father. Joey's movie career was spotty, to say the least, but she was a sought-after performer on the nightclub circuits for many years.

MAN CRAZY

starring

NEVILLE BRAND
CHRISTINE WHITE
IRENE ANDERS
COLEEN MILLER
JOHN BROWN

Written and Produced by

SIDNEY HARMON

and

PHILIP YORDAN

Directed by

IRVING LERNER

A
Security Pictures Production.
Released by
20th Century-Fox

A restless brunette, played by Coleen Miller (1932–), and her two pals head to Hollywood with piles of loot that don't belong to them in order to make it in the big city in *Man Crazy* (Security Pictures, 1953). Here Coleen (left) falls in with the wrong kind of guy, played by the ubiquitous Neville Brand, as her conniving roommate (Christine White, 1932–) looks on. Coleen went on to costar in a number of colorful Westerns, but her film career was already winding down by the end of the decade.

TEENAGE REBEL
CINEMASCOPE
GINGER ROGERS · MICHAEL RENNIE
and Three Stars of the Future
BETTY LOU KEIM · WARREN BERLINGER · DIANE JERGENS
CHARLES BRACKETT · EDMUND GOULDING · WALTER REISCH · CHARLES BRACKETT

Ginger Rogers (1911–95) was certainly no stranger to playing an occasional bad girl in a film career that spanned four decades, but the tables were turned in the cheesy *Teenage Rebel* (Fox, 1956). Betty Lou Keim (1938–) played the troubled teen who raises hell when she comes to live with her divorced mom, who is newly remarried. Betty Lou was voted a Star of the Future by the Fox publicity machine, but she never lived up to the hype.

Susan Oliver (1932–90) played a lot of proper, comely young ladies from good families, so it was a nice treat when a director allowed her to tap into a more sinister side. *The Green-Eyed Blonde* (Warner Bros., 1957) was one such departure for Susan and she pulled out all the stops as a seductive young rebel who gets involved in a murder and suffers the appropriate bad-girl ending for her rotten deeds.

Mere words cannot describe *Bayou* (United Artists, 1957), a masterpiece of bad filmmaking, starring the always sultry Lita Milan (1933–) as a backwoods Cajun hellcat who wants a better life. Her prayers may be answered in the form of a visiting architect (clean-cut Peter Graves) and it's lust at first sight. However, the brutish Tim Carey (pictured) isn't giving Lita up without a fight. This gem was released again a few years later under the even more sensational title, *Poor White Trash*.

Diane McBain (1941–) was a stunning blonde contract player who was a much better actress than films like *Claudelle Inglish* (Warner Bros., 1961) warranted. In it, Diane is an overheated Southern head-turner who becomes a trashy slut when she's jilted by her boyfriend. Here she fends off the attention of a well-to-do clod, (Arthur Kennedy) who desires her. *Claudelle Inglish* was a box office disappointment, and Diane's career slid even further in more unworthy vehicles like *The Miniskirt Mob* and *Maryjane*; about an all-girl biker gang and marijuana addiction, respectively.

COLUMBIA PICTURES
AND SAM SPIEGEL PRESENT "The"

HAPPENING

ANTHONY QUINN · MICHAEL PARKS · GEORGE MAHARIS
ROBERT WALKER · MARTHA HYER AND INTRODUCING FAYE DUNAWAY
CO-STARRING OSCAR HOMOLKA · JACK KRUSCHEN · MILTON BERLE as Fred

A HORIZON PICTURE TECHNICOLOR®

Three young thugs — George Maharis, Michael Parks, and Faye Dunaway (in her film debut) — kidnap the crude yet wealthy Anthony Quinn and hold him for ransom in *The Happening* (Columbia, 1967). Faye (1941–) made quite a splash as her first big screen bad girl and it wouldn't be the last such role in the Oscar winner's long, impressive career, which still shows no sign of slowing down.

Every time Alain Delon kisses Lola Albright, he wonders if she wants to kiss him or kill him.

Metro-Goldwyn-Mayer
presents
"JOY HOUSE"

A gigolo (Alain Delon) seeks refuge in a foreboding French château inhabited by two mysterious women — Lola Albright (1925–) and Jane Fonda, in an early screen appearance — who keep him around as a love slave. The appropriately titled *Joy House* (MGM, 1964) was ahead of its time and the theme a little too risqué (and bizarre) for U.S. audiences. Here we see a chic Lola — a vastly underrated actress — slowly killing Alain with her kisses!

Susan Cabot (1927–86) was not without talent, but producers continued to waste her in unworthy (though no less amusing) efforts like *Sorority Girl* (A.I.P., 1957), one of the six pictures she made for director Roger Corman.

At 30, she played the title role as Sabra, an alienated rich girl who bring misery to her fellow college "sisters."

By 1960, Susan's film career was over (*Wasp Woman* was her final feature), and she became something of a recluse. In 1986 she was beaten to death by her son inside their decaying Hollywood mansion. (JC Archives)

Vivacious Carole Landis (1919–48) starred as a socialite with a checkered past who is implicated in the murder of a blackmailer in *Behind Green Lights* (Fox, 1946), costarring veteran character actor William Gargan. Carole, a famous WWII pinup girl, was sadly wasted in minor films for most of her career. After four failed marriages she embarked on a disastrous love affair with actor Rex Harrison, which was mentioned as the reason for her suicide in 1948 at the age of twenty-nine.

Plucky Lola Lane (1909–81) is determined to find out *Why Girls Leave Home* (PRC, 1945), an entertaining antique centering around the alleged suicide of a nightclub singer. The trail leads her to a dive called The Kitten Club, where she earns the trust of a hard-drinking vocalist played by Claudia Drake (1918–97), and helps to expose an illegal gambling ring. Both Lane (seated) and Drake (standing) were old pros who supplied many well-delivered wisecracks in dozens of B movies in the 1930s and 1940s.

A thrill-seeking teenager (Lowell Brown) gets involved with a cheap diner waitress — the curvy Joyce Meadows (1937?–) — which leads him down a dangerous road in *The Girl in Lovers Lane* (Filmgroup Inc., 1960) a grade-Z chiller that, not surprisingly, did very little to advance the lovely Joyce into the major leagues.

For a brief moment in time, Edy Williams (1942–) was poised to become a major movie sex goddess, especially under the guidance of her then husband, legendary producer/director Russ Meyer, but that kind of megastardom would allude her, and *Beyond the Valley of the Dolls* (Russ Meyer Productions/Fox, 1970) remains the most famous of Edy's films. Here Edy (as predatory porn star Ashley St. Ives) prepares to make a sexual smorgasbord of costar David Gurian. Having never met a flashbulb she didn't like, Edy still manages to turn heads on the red carpet, often wearing the least amount of fabric allowed by law. (JC Archives)

COLUMBIA PICTURES Presents

A JOHN FRANKENHEIMER—EDWARD LEWIS Production

starring

GREGORY PECK
TUESDAY WELD
ESTELLE PARSONS

I WALK THE LINE

co-starring

RALPH MEEKER · Screenplay by ALVIN SARGENT
Based on the novel "An Exile" by MADISON JONES
Music by JOHNNY CASH · Produced by HAROLD D. COHEN
Executive Producer EDWARD LEWIS · Directed by JOHN FRANKENHEIMER

PANAVISION® COLOR   GP   C

In the oddly fascinating *I Walk the Line* (Columbia, 1970), Tuesday Weld (1943–) is the fetching daughter of a backwoods moonshiner and Gregory Peck is the small-town sheriff who flips for her, though he should know better. Tuesday had sex appeal to spare but she also had the talent to back it up, a commodity in short supply in 1950s and 1960s Hollywood. Her characters could be soft and sentimental, but beware: they could also be selfish, manipulative, and rotten-to-the-core if provoked. Tuesday was nominated for an Oscar for *Looking for Mr. Goodbar* in 1977.

No cinema bad girl was ever so unstable as the wealthy Ellen Berent, played by Gene Tierney (1920–91), in *Leave Her to Heaven* (Fox, 1945), a rare film noir that was shot in glorious Technicolor. In the name of love (or her very warped perception of it) for her new husband (Cornel Wilde), Gene coldly watches her brother drown, causes her own miscarriage, and ultimately poisons herself in order to implicate her sister! Quite a handful indeed for the usually more demure Gene, who received an Academy Award nomination for her performance. (JC Archives)

Susan Hayward (1918–75) does a perfect job of chewing the scenery in *I Can Get It for You Wholesale* (Fox, 1951), a dated morality play about a ruthless fashion designer who uses very questionable ethics in her dizzying climb to the top of the garment biz. Character actress Mary Philips plays Hayward's mother who disapproves of her daughter's scandalous behavior. (JC Archives)

20th
CENTURY-FOX
presents

INFERNO
Technicolor

Starring
ROBERT RYAN · RHONDA FLEMING · WILLIAM LUNDIGAN

with LARRY KEATING · HENRY HULL · CARL BETZ · ROBERT BURTON

Produced by WILLIAM BLOOM · Directed by ROY BAKER · Written by FRANCIS COCKRELL

Rhonda Fleming (1923–) is at her most duplicitous as she callously plans to do away with her rich husband (Robert Ryan) by leaving him to die in the desert in *Inferno* (Fox, 1953). Plot twists abound in this effective thriller, which was originally released in 3-D and costarred William Lundigan (seen here with the greedy Rhonda).

Jennifer Jones (1919–) pulled out all the stops as trashy Southern hellcat *Ruby Gentry* (Paramount, 1952) who married for money but carries on a torrid love affair with Charlton Heston, which, of course, leads to some serious consequences. This scene shows Jennifer and Charlton getting quite literally down and dirty in this campy melodrama.

While in London, an unfaithful American actress, Gloria Grahame (1924–81), attracts the attention of a handsome opportunist (Lee Patterson) who involves her husband in a plot to rob a cash-filled postal van in *The Good Die Young* (Romulus, 1954). Gloria was very adept at playing fallen women and cheats, and gave a strong performance in the film, though ultimately even she couldn't salvage the mediocre material. She nabbed a Best Supporting Actress Oscar two years earlier for her role in *The Bad and the Beautiful.*

Jean Simmons (1929–) played the title role in *Hilda Crane* (Fox, 1956) about a woman with two divorces already under her belt who returns to the small town she grew up in and proceeds to set tongues wagging with her scandalous behavior. Jean Pierre Aumont costarred in this rather predictable soap opera, which was surprisingly not redeemed by another good performance by Jean.

Authentic Manhattan locations highlight *Close-Up* (Eagle Lion Films, 1948), a nail-biting little thriller about a dangerous band of Nazi criminals in postwar New York City. Virginia Gilmore (1919–86) plays a sinister member of the gang that tries to silence an innocent man who inadvertently uncovers their nefarious deeds. Virginia (who was married to Yul Brynner from 1944–60) didn't have a long career in pictures but spent many years on the stage and later became a drama coach. (JC Archives)

The triangle is about to explode, as Julie (Gina Lollobrigida) stands between the two men in her life.

M-G-M presents
An Arcola Production

"GO NAKED IN THE WORLD"

CinemaScope
Metrocolor

In *Go Naked in the World* (Arcola/MGM, 1960) a jubilant soldier (Anthony Franciosa) from a wealthy family introduces his fiancée played by Gina Lollobrigida (1927–) to his parents (Nancy R. Pollock and Ernest Borgnine), unaware that she is a famous San Francisco call girl who once counted his father (Borgnine, right) as one of her customers! The sets and costumes (designer Helen Rose outdid herself on Gina's duds) got the best reviews in this dull yet lavish soap opera.

A respected London psychiatrist (Robert Newton) has his hands full with his cheating wife, played by Sally Gray (1916–), so he cleverly turns the tables on his unfaithful spouse in *The Hidden Room* (Eagle Lion Films, 1949). Sally entered films in 1930 while still a teenager, specializing in portraying wise-cracking blondes. After only two more films she married into the British aristocracy and retired from films completely. (JC Archives)

Voluptuous starlet Lila Leeds (1928–) was an up-and-coming actress when she was arrested for marijuana possession in 1948 after a raid on her Hollywood bungalow. Part of Lila's court-ordered sentence was to make an antidrug movie called *Wild Weed* (Eureka/Jewel, 1949), which is about a chorus girl who ruins her career by smoking dope. The film (costarring Alan Baxter) became a cult favorite on the midnight-movie circuit under the alternate titles *The Devil's Weed* and *She Should'a Said No*. Coincidentally Robert Mitchum was also arrested at Lila's cottage but his career was unaffected by the scandal; the same can't be said for Lila's. (JC Archives)

PORTRAIT STILL

HIT and RUN

STARRING
CLEO MOORE · HUGO HAAS · VINCE EDWARDS
Written, Produced and Directed by HUGO HAAS
Released thru UNITED ARTISTS

Trashy double-crossing Cleo Moore (1928–73) plots to rid herself of her unsuspecting husband (Hugo Haas) with the help of her lover (Vince Edwards, in his pre-Ben Casey days) in *Hit and Run* (United Artists, 1957). Cleo had a lock on these lurid melodramas in the 1950s, often under the direction of Haas (they did seven pictures together) before retiring in 1957. The former film siren ran for governor of Louisiana in 1973 but was defeated. No doubt she would have added some spice to that office!

A WWII vet (Don Taylor) returns home with a *Japanese War Bride* (Fox, 1952) only to encounter racism in his community. Marie Windsor (1919–2000), one of cinema's most underrated actresses, played his vicious, judgmental sister-in-law in this well acted B picture. (JC Archives)

SCENE STILL

Arlene Dahl (1924–) makes another indelible impression as a big screen bad girl in *Wicked as They Come* (Columbia, 1956), a nicely done British picture about a beautiful, ambitious woman from the seedy part of town who stops at nothing (even murder) to get what she wants. Phil Carey and Totti Truman-Taylor (as a kindly nun) lend some comfort to Arlene, but it may be too late for this Dahl (pun intended).

COLUMBIA PICTURES presents
ARLENE DAHL · PHIL CAREY
HERBERT MARSHALL
WICKED AS THEY COME

LOBBY CARD

SEVENTEEN and LONESOME

TAMING SUTTON'S GAL

IN NATURAMA

Hollywood had a long history of crossing over to the wrong side of the tracks in search of fresh bad girl story lines, but regretfully the plots were usually tired tales seen a hundred times before. That's certainly the case with *Taming Sutton's Gal* (Republic, 1957) with Gloria Talbott (1931–2000) as the love-starved wife of a hillbilly moonshiner. Gloria became a fan favorite in 1950s horror drivel like *The Daughter of Dr. Jekyll* and *I Married a Monster from Outer Space*.

DOUBLE IDENTITY!

DOUBLE-CROSS!

FRAME-UP!..
...Sparked by sinister "sister act."

Harvard Film Corp. presents

DEADLY DUO

starring
CRAIG HILL · MARCIA HENDERSON · ROBERT LOWERY
Produced by ROBERT E. KENT · Directed by REGINALD LeBORG
Screenplay by OWEN HARRIS · From the novel by RICHARD JESSUP
Released thru UNITED **UA** ARTISTS

Deadly Duo (Harvard Film Corp., 1962) wasn't a terrible movie, but it suffered from a dreadfully minuscule budget. Marcia Henderson (1929–87) played nasty twin sisters who involve gullible Craig Hill in a dangerous insurance scam. Marcia won the 1950 Theatre World Award for a production of *Peter Pan* (she was Wendy) and honed her craft in the early days of live television before giving motion pictures a try. Sadly she was underappreciated (remember *The Wayward Girl* or *Riot in Juvenile Prison*?) and called it a day after only fourteen films.

Emotions run wild as a trio of murky characters face off in a snowbound cabin in *High Hell* (Paramount, 1958). Elaine Stewart (1929–) plays the unfaithful wife of a mine owner who flaunts her affair with his handsome business partner (John Derek). Elaine solidified her femme fatale status in this claustrophobic British melodrama that features a scene with the sexy Elaine bathing in a rain barrel.

HIGH HELL

STARRING
JOHN DEREK
ELAINE STEWART

PRODUCED BY
BURT BALABAN AND ARTHUR MAYER

BURT BALABAN · IRVE TUNICK · STEVE FRAZEE

A PRINCESS PRODUCTION · PARAMOUNT RELEASE

A wealthy vineyard owner (Rod Steiger) has good reason to suspect that his cheap wife, played by Diana Dors (1931–84), is up to no good in the mediocre melodrama *The Unholy Wife* (RKO, 1957). Already a sex symbol in her native England, Diana hoped to duplicate that success in America, but the film, directed by John Farrow (yep, Mia's dad), was a flop. Returning to Great Britain, Diana continued to milk her blonde-bombshell image long after the luster had faded. By the mid-1960s, weight gain (and a shifting popularity) forced her into more mature parts, where she remained (quite effectively) until her death from cancer.

CRIME AGAINST JOE
He Was Accused Of The Foulest Act A Man Can Commit!

JOHN BROMFIELD
JULIE LONDON · HENRY CALVIN

John Bromfield and Julie London (1926–2000) supplied the heat in the above-average drama *Crime Against Joe* (United Artists, 1956). Julie is wonderful as Slacks, a hard-boiled carhop who sets out to help her guy when he gets framed for murder. Julie juggled her film work with a red-hot recording career, which went on to include thirty-two albums.

CHAPTER FIVE

FOREIGN BODIES

In America sex is an obsession; in the rest of the world it is a fact.
—Marlene Dietrich

INSELTOWN has had a long, but not always laudable, history with the actresses it has imported for various film work. In the sound-free 1920s a foreign-born actress wasn't limited to playing only sloe-eyed vamps, but this changed with the advent of the talkies. Suddenly a Russian, Polish, or German accent became a liability when audible dialogue was essential to the plot. Anything external was immediately equated with the exotic, and very few of these women could break through that barrier. An example was the beautiful Lupe Velez, who played a wide variety of roles in silent movies, in which her ethnicity wasn't an issue. All that changed with the arrival of sound, and suddenly the Mexican-born star was reduced to playing half-castes and fiery gypsies, or worse, grotesque lampoons of those roles. Some, like Greta Garbo and Marlene Dietrich, were exceptions to the rule, but even with their enormous popularity, an air of mystery permeated their work and the publicity that surrounded it.

The postwar attitude changed very slowly. Dozens of French, Italian, and Scandinavian starlets were typically used as nothing more than dark and brooding set dressing. Happily, the European film industry was becoming a hub of activity, attracting distributors from all over the world, which gave their product a much wider audience. This new attention brought these ladies fame on an international level that was crucial to their success. If they tired of playing sexy counterspies in American films, there were now more opportunities abroad. Most of these foreign bodies fared much better on their home turf anyway, while others like Brigitte Bardot and Maria Felix declined to work in Hollywood at all. Actually the overseas markets have been much more protective of their artists (especially the ones over thirty-five), as reflected by their lengthy filmographies. So it is to this bevy of beauteous bad girls that we tip our *chapeaux. Brava bella!*

COLUMBIA PICTURES presents

BRIGITTE BARDOT
"LA VÉRITÉ"

CHARLES VANEL · PAUL MEURISSE

Written and Directed by
HENRI-GEORGES CLOUZOT

Produced by RAOUL J. LEVY

Brigitte Bardot (1934–) is on trial for the murder of her lover (who was also her sister's fiancé) in the French film *La Vérité* (Iena/CEIAP, 1960). Though Brigitte has not appeared on screen for more than thirty years, she is still a national treasure in her native France. She achieved international superstardom with the release of *And God Created Woman* in 1956, directed by her then husband Roger Vadim. Together they introduced the world to a new kind of sex symbol. Still kittenish in the older Hollywood tradition, Brigitte also displayed an independent sensuality that was perfectly timed with the sexual revolution of the 1960s. Some of BB's (as she is sometimes addressed in the press) more sensational films were *The Bride Is Much Too Beautiful*, *Love Is My Profession*, *Love on a Pillow*, and *A Very Private Affair*. The legend now devotes most of her time to animal rights causes.

PARAMOUNT PICTURES PRESENTS **SOPHIA LOREN · TAB HUNTER**

That Kind Of Woman

CO STARRING

JACK WARDEN

BARBARA NICHOLS

KEENAN WYNN

ALSO CO STARRING

GEORGE SANDERS AS THE MAN

PRODUCED BY CARLO PONTI AND MARCELLO GIROSI   DIRECTED BY SIDNEY LUMET   SCREENPLAY BY WALTER BERNSTEIN   BASED ON A STORY BY ROBERT LOWRY

Sophia Loren (1934–) was right on the verge of international stardom (after nine years in Italian cinema) when she became *That Kind of Woman* (Paramount, 1959) for director Sidney Lumet. Sophia plays a fallen woman who tumbles for an American soldier (a miscast Tab Hunter) while on a train trip. The movie was filmed originally with Nancy Carroll in 1929, and again with Margaret Sullavan in 1938 under the title *Shopworn Angel*.

J. ARTHUR RANK presents

GOOD TIME GIRL

Starring

**JEAN KENT
DENNIS PRICE
FLORA ROBSON
GRIFFITH JONES
HERBERT LOM**

EAGLE-LION

Jean Kent (1921–) was so good at playing vicious trouble-makers that she quickly became typecast in those roles. Here the British-born actress causes problems for poor Herbert Lom in *Good Time Girl* (Rank, 1948), a film about a wayward hussy who learns a valuable lesson in life just in the nick of time. After nearly forty films, Jean remained active on the London stage for many years.

Long before *Dynasty* (1981–89) recharged her career, Joan Collins (1933–) appeared in many films in her native England and in the United States, including *Turn the Key Softly* (Rank, 1953), a minor British drama centering around the lives of a group of paroled female convicts. Here Collins (third from the left) and fellow parolees Yvonne Mitchell (1925–79, second from left) and Dorothy Alison (1925–95, far right) admire an old pal's new trinket.

Any Man…
Any Place…
Any Time!

Gina Lollobrigida

The LONELY WOMAN

A bored (and married) photo-grapher, played by Gina Lollobrigida (1927–), embarks on an affair with an opportunistic young man (Renaud Verley) in *The Lonely Woman* (Independent-International, 1972), unaware that her husband has a mistress of his own in this confusing European sizzler. The film also marked Gina's last theatrical motion picture and was released in Italy under the alternate title *Mortal Sin.*

Before Sophia Loren and Gina Lollobrigida, there was Silvana Mangano (1930–89), a former Miss Rome in 1946 who became a famous sex symbol during the Italian film industry's neo-realism period, often in unrestrained, highly erotic roles. *Gold of Naples* (DCA, 1954) was a film (directed by Vittorio De Sica) in which Silvana played a sensitive prostitute in a very unconventional marriage. Silvana was married to producer Dino De Laurentiis from 1949 until her death from cancer forty years later.

A mysterious brunette with cat-like features, Barbara Shelley (1933–) supplied sufficient menace to dozens of British thrillers and atmospheric horror movies, including *Man in the Dark* (Universal, 1965), with William Sylvester as an innocent sap who gets involved in a web of murder and deceit thanks to a double-dealing vixen (Barbara). She later played similar roles on television in the United States and in her native England.

COLUMBIA PICTURES presents
STEWART GRANGER
DONNA REED
GEORGE SANDERS
"THE WHOLE
TRUTH"
and
introducing
GIANNA MARIA CANALE

A dark, alluring Italian beauty (who could resist that gaze?) Gianna Maria Canale (1927–) lent considerable smolder to the British mystery *The Whole Truth* (Columbia, 1958). She specialized in portraying temptresses in scores of low-budget costume spectacles for more than two decades, including *I Vampiri*, in which her evil countess character bathed in the blood of innocent maidens.

CINEMASCOPE
EASTMANCOLOR

ULTRA PICTURES PRESENTS

ELSA MARTINELLI IN RICE GIRL

A CARLO PONTI-EXCELSA PRODUCTION · RELEASED BY ULTRA PICTURES CORP A BELLOTTI FILM

Elsa Martinelli (1932–) came to films by way of the fashion industry, where she walked the runway as a top mannequin before being discovered by Kirk Douglas for his Western *The Indian Fighter* in 1955. Returning to her native Italy she starred in *Rice Girl* (Ultra Pictures, 1956) for famed producer Carlo Ponti as a field worker with a murky past. She has since starred in numerous motion pictures of many nations while enjoying a busy social life as one of the world's beautiful people.

The Racers (Fox, 1955) was the third film for Bella Darvi (1927–71), seen here with Kirk Douglas, under her personal contract with Hollywood mogul Darryl F. Zanuck. Like her first two bids for stardom (the clinker *Hell and High Water* and the ten-ton biblical epic *The Egyptian*) it did not go over well with ticket buyers, and the Polish-born former model headed back to the playgrounds of Europe. There Bella played sexy leads (usually as femme fatales) in several dreadful productions and spent most of her free time (and money) in casinos along the Riviera, incurring large gambling debts. Despondent, she took her own life in 1971 in her Monte Carlo apartment by opening the gas jets on the stove. Her final folderol, *Good Little Girls*, was released that year.

THE RACERS

Produced by · Directed by · Screen Play by
JULIAN BLAUSTEIN · HENRY HATHAWAY · CHARLES KAUFMAN

LOBBY CARD

The Shakedown

starring
TERENCE MORGAN
HAZEL COURT
and
ROBERT BEATTY

Original Story and Screenplay
LEIGH VANCE and JOHN LEMONT

Directed by JOHN LEMONT

Produced by NORMAN WILLIAM

Alliance Film Distributors
Limited Production

A Universal-International
Release

LOBBY CARD

The Shakedown (Alliance Films, 1960) was a hilarious bit of exploitation concerning a blackmail ring headed by the sleazy Terence Morgan, who preys on the students of a low-rent photography school. The luscious Hazel Court (1926–) pays the hush money so her nude photos won't surface and ruin her modeling career. Hazel became a fan favorite in a series of atmospheric horror movies in the 1950s and 1960s but retired from films in 1964 after a deliciously evil role in *The Masque of the Red Death*, an Edgar Allen Poe tale.

LOBBY CARD

A Kentucky truck driver (James Franciscus) heads to New York City in search of fame and fortune as a writer, and becomes the sexual plaything of a spoiled, predatory socialite in *Youngblood Hawke* (Warner Bros., 1964). Parisian Genevieve Page (1930–) was the chic yet neurotic beauty who supplies ample chaos to the young novelist's life in this trashy guilty pleasure. Genevieve worked infrequently in the United States, but starred in more than forty films in her native France (as well as in Germany and Italy), where she is still in demand.

Judy Geeson (1948–) made an easy transition from playing teenage delinquents (*To Sir, with Love*) to simmering British sex kittens in dozens of comedies and horror films in the 1960s. Here Judy is trying to claim another victim (Michael Gough) in *Berserk!* (Columbia, 1967), in which she played a psycho killer bumping off members of a traveling circus run by none other than Joan Crawford who played her mother!

After several European films (none very memorable) the Swedish-born May Britt (1933–) was chosen to play Lola-Lola (immortalized by Marlene Dietrich in the original) in the highly publicized remake of *The Blue Angel* (Fox, 1959). Curt Jurgens (pictured) played the prudish professor whose life is ruined by the amoral cabaret star. The film was savaged by the critics and nearly destroyed May's career, so she retired to concentrate on married life (she wed singer Sammy Davis Jr. in 1960) and motherhood. After their marriage ended in the late 1960s, she returned to acting in several international motion pictures.

Before assuming the role of Miss Moneypenny in fourteen James Bond adventures, Canadian-born Lois Maxwell (1927–) had a long career in British, Italian, and American films. *The Big Punch* (Warner Bros., 1948) was a stylish Hollywood thriller about a boxer falsely accused of a homicide. Here Lois, as a shady lady, confers with gangster Marc Logan about the fighter's whereabouts. (JC Archives)

Busty blonde British glamour girl Sandra Dorne (1925–92) was never more wicked than as the avaricious mistress of a novelist (Tony Wright, pictured) in *The House in Marsh Road* (Grand National, 1960). Together they arrange the murder of his naive wife, but things don't go according to plan. Sandra provided substantial steam to almost four dozen films but never became a top-rank star. Her on-screen appearances dwindled considerably by the mid-1960s. (JC Archives)

A two-timing gun moll, played by Anita Ekberg (1931–), pays a steep price for her treachery when she tries to cheat a violent hoodlum (Berry Kroeger) out of a cash-filled safety deposit box in *Man in the Vault* (RKO, 1956). The Swedish starlet was a newcomer in Hollywood when she made this undistinguished B picture, one of several made in the United States before she returned to Europe and greater worldwide fame.

"MAN IN THE VAULT"

WILLIAM CAMPBELL · KAREN SHARPE · ANITA EKBERG

Luciana Paluzzi (1931–), pictured here with Robert Vaughn in the espionage caper *To Trap A Spy* (MGM, 1966), never became a household name, but it wasn't for lack of trying. After her motion picture debut in 1954, the Italian-born Luciana worked regularly all over the world, most notably as a James Bond villainess in *Thunderball* and as a vamp who lures Frankie away from Annette (temporarily of course) in *Muscle Beach Party*. She also starred on the television series *Five Fingers* in 1960 as a beautiful fashion model involved with enemy Communist agents in Europe.

Nr. 28 / 22. JAHRGANG 1952

Mein film

2 SCHILLING

In Deutschland 35 D-Pfennig
Übriges Ausland 15 Dollarcents

Silvana Pampanini
In dem Film „Weiße Sklavon"
Photo: Willan

Aus dem Inhalt 1. Bildbericht über den Osterreich-Film / Helmut Käutner gibt
dieser Nummer: nicht auf / Tausend rote Rosen blühen / Pier Angeli am Trapez

The uninhibited Silvana Pampanini (1925–), a former Miss Italy, may not have scaled the professional heights of Sophia Loren or Gina Lollobrigida, but she was one of Italy's first postwar sex symbols who kept flashbulbs popping and hearts racing for decades. Reduced almost immediately to the B-ranks after her 1946 film debut, Silvana was nevertheless a wildly popular star and a favorite magazine cover girl, as illustrated here on *Mein Film* (Germany, January 1952). Some of her more than sixty films include the provocatively titled *Don Juan's Night of Love*, *The Island Sinner*, *The Woman Who Invented Love*, *Girls Marked Danger*, *Law of the Streets*, and *Thirst for Love*.

Mary Had a Little (Lopert, 1961), a low-rent sex comedy, boasted a provocative title but little else. French starlet Agnes Laurent (1935–) was a shapely newlywed who is just a little too free-spirited for her own good. Agnes made a few pictures in the swinging 1960s (almost all in her native France), but not too many people flocked to see *Soft Skin on Black Silk* or *Dictionary of Love* and her career was a brief one.

The beautiful Anna Sten (1908–93) was already a film star in Russia (where she was born) and Germany when she came to the attention of megaproducer Sam Goldwyn, who brought her to Hollywood with the hope of turning her into another Garbo. He starred Anna as a doomed courtesan in the film version of *Nana* in 1934, based on the story by Emile Zola. It bombed at the box office (as did her subsequent pictures, *We Live Again*, also in 1934, and *The Wedding Night* in 1935), and Goldwyn's "passionate peasant" (as she was dubbed by the studio press agents) slipped quietly into B movies like the hilariously titled *They Came to Blow Up America*. She later became a respected painter and had exhibitions of her work around the world.

Pola NEGRI

Pola Negri (1894–1987) started appearing in silent films in her native Poland and later in Germany before Hollywood beckoned, making her one of the screen's most exotic beauties. However, with the advent of sound her thick Polish accent became a hindrance, and those heavy, dramatic femme fatale roles were proving less than popular with audiences, so she returned to Europe where movie offers were still plentiful. Pola did take an occasional part in the United States, her last being *The Moon-Spinners* in 1964, again as a villainess.

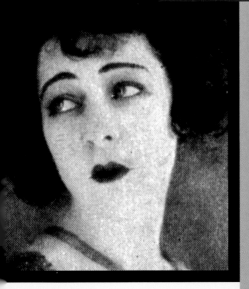

Brooding and distant Alla Nazimova (1879–1945) emigrated from what was then Crimea in Russia and began appearing in silent films in 1916 after a period on the Moscow stage. Dubbed The Woman of a Thousand Moods by a savvy public relations team, Alla's very dramatic acting style was well suited to the vehicles she starred in (and occasionally produced), such as *Toys of Fate, Eye for Eye, Madame Peacock, Madonna of the Streets*, and a bizarre, highly erotic version of *Camille* costarring Rudolph Valentino. Her sexuality was the source of much gossip during her movie career, which lasted until she retired in 1925. Nazimova (she was sometimes billed using just her last name) returned to pictures in 1940 in a series of memorable character parts.

POUR VOUS

NUMÉRO 586
7 FÉVRIER 1940

TOUS LES MERCREDIS
UN FRANC 75

Turbulente et langoureuse à la fois, LUPE VELEZ, la pittoresque vedette mexicaine de Hollywood, vient d'achever un nouveau film.

FOREIGN MAGAZINE

Much like Anna May Wong, who started at roughly the same time, Lupe Velez (1905–44) quickly discovered that the ethnicities Hollywood originally found appealing could become a career prison. This was the industry that the Mexican-born Lupe, seen here on the cover of *Pour Vous* (France, 1940), found in 1927 when she was cast opposite Douglas Fairbanks in *The Gaucho*. She was soon relegated to playing fiery, hell-raising peasant girls in dozens of films. Eventually even those roles became garish caricatures (as in RKO's *Mexican Spitfire* and its seven sequels). Frustrated with her professional and personal choices, Lupe prepared a lavish suicide, complete with a grand farewell supper. She downed seventy-five Seconal tablets, but the result was not what she expected. Apparently still woozy from her pills, Lupe staggered to her bathroom, where she was discovered by her maid the following morning. She had drowned in her chartruese, marble commode — a tragic finale that has become the stuff of show-biz legend.

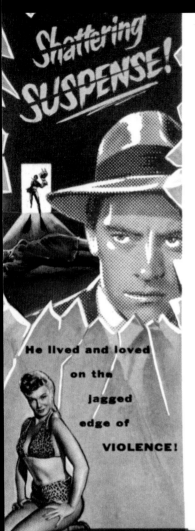

John Ireland finds a mess of trouble in a seedy traveling carnival in the mystery *The Glass Tomb* (Lippert, 1955), costarring the sexy powder keg Honor Blackman (1925–), who paid her dues in more than two dozen films before becoming perhaps the quintessential Bond girl, Pussy Galore, in *Goldfinger* (1965). If that wasn't enough, Honor starred on *The Avengers* for three years (1962–65) as the take-no-prisoners Cathy Gale before leaving to pursue more movie work (Diana Rigg replaced her in the cast). These two roles earned her legions of fans and a die-hard cult following.

SEVEN ARTS PRODUCTIONS Presents
AGATHA CHRISTIE'S CLASSIC MYSTERY

TEN LITTLE INDIANS

THE WHODUNIT BREAK!
A FIRST IN MOVIES! SIXTY SECONDS FOR YOU TO GUESS THE KILLER!

HUGH O'BRIAN / SHIRLEY EATON / FABIAN / LEO GENN / STANLEY HOLLOWAY / MARIANNE HOPPE
WILFRID HYDE-WHITE / DALIAH LAVI / DENNIS PRICE and MARIO ADORF in "TEN LITTLE INDIANS"

Produced by OLIVER A. UNGER Directed by GEORGE POLLOCK Screenplay by PETER YELDHAM & PETER WELBECK
Produced in association with HARRY M. POPKIN A SEVEN ARTS PICTURES RELEASE

Shirley Eaton (1936–), another saucy English lass, decorated a number of ribald British comedies, including three in the legendary *Carry On* series, and is seen here as one of several suspected murderers in the whodunit *Ten Little Indians* (Seven Arts, 1966), based on the Agatha Christie mystery. Shirley is best remembered as the gold-painted body (and what a body) in *Goldfinger* (1965) which made her famous on an international scale.

Rome wasn't built in a day...but

these four beautiful women tore it apart in a night!

GIANNI HECHT LUCARI

Ursula **Andress**
Virna **Lisi**
Anyone Can Play
Claudine **Auger**

Jean-Pierre **Cassel** Frank **Wolff** Lando **Buzzanca** Mario **Adorf** Marisa **Mell**

EXECUTIVE PRODUCER FAUSTO SARACENI DIRECTED BY LUIGI ZAMPA

ONE SHEET POSTER

A quartet of Europe's sexiest dolls
— Ursula Andress (Swiss, 1936–),
Virna Lisi (Italian, 1937–), Claudine
Auger (a former Miss France, 1942–),
and Marisa Mell (Austrian, 1939–92)
— took Rome (and every man in it) by
storm in *Anyone Can Play* (Paramount,
1968), a scorching tale of love, lust,
and adultery in the Eternal City.

The nonsensical *A Witch Without a Broom* (PRO, 1967), a Spanish comedy, received very few bookings in the United States except for those on the drive-in circuit. It starred 1950s heartthrob Jeffrey Hunter and Austrian beauty Maria Perschy (1938–) as the groovy sorceress in question. Maria was rarely offscreen in the 1960s and early 1970s, appearing in countless European productions with scant clothing and exploitative female titles such as *Seven Vengeful Women*, *Isle of Lost Women*, and *The House of Psychotic Women*. (Is this a theme?)

A VERY HEXY MOTION PICTURE!

SHE'S BEWITCHED!
She's Hexciting!

Here's a switch on a witch—
she's in love and going all the way
from the Stone Age to the Space Age
as romance mixes up her brew!

starring
Jeffrey Hunter
Maria Perschy

A Witch Without a Broom in COLOR

Produced by Sidney Pink Directed by Joe Lacy color by Movielab A PRO Release

ONE SHEET POSTER

A handsome cad (Jacques Sernas) puts the moves on a sexy foreign exchange student in the trashy *Luxury Girls* (Cines, 1953). The British-born Susan Stephen (1931–2000) is the pouty coed who is corrupted by all sorts of shocking behavior at an exclusive boarding school. Susan's husky voice served her well in a series of crime dramas and adventure films, but her roles declined sharply by the early 1960s.

In postwar France, Françoise Arnoul (1931–) became an enormously admired young actress who specialized in portraying tempestuous, sexually liberated teenagers (or as the poster promised, "a girl who couldn't control her emotions") in steamy dramas such as *Sin and Desire* (Atlantis Films, 1960). Algerian-born Françoise played a variation on that theme into adulthood, but she remained mostly unknown in American markets despite appearing in more than eighty films abroad.

THE STORY OF A GIRL WHO COULDN'T CONTROL HER EMOTIONS!!

FRANCOISE ARNOUL *IN* SIN & DESIRE

An Atlantis Films Inc. release

LOBBY CARD

As soon as a rhinestone crown was placed on a pretty girl's head there seemed to be a movie producer waiting with a contract. This was the case with the beautiful Nadja Tiller (1929–), who burst upon the scene shortly after being named Miss Austria in 1949. Nadja toiled in small parts for a decade until she landed the title role in *Rosemary* (Films-Around-The-World, 1958), the true story of a Frankfurt call girl who knew too much and loses her life because of it. The frank and scandalous (at the time) film made Nadja an international sex kitten, and she was linked to the character for many years, being dubbed "that *Rosemary* girl" in all her press.

"A steamy item— this rueful reflection on the fleshpots" – *Crowther, N.Y. Times*

ROSEMARY

introducing in the title role Nadja Tiller with Peter Van Eyck
Story by Erich Kuby · Directed by Rolf Thiele · Produced by Luggi Waldleitner
Released by FILMS AROUND THE WORLD

ORIGINAL PRESS BOOK

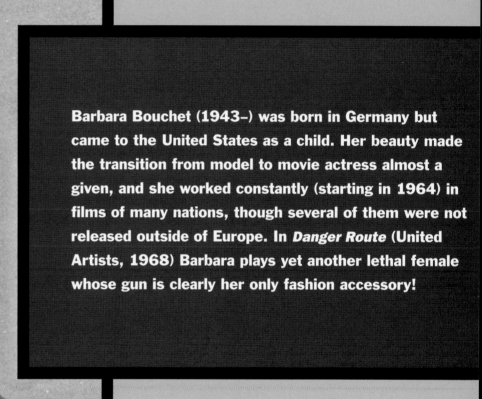

Barbara Bouchet (1943–) was born in Germany but came to the United States as a child. Her beauty made the transition from model to movie actress almost a given, and she worked constantly (starting in 1964) in films of many nations, though several of them were not released outside of Europe. In *Danger Route* (United Artists, 1968) Barbara plays yet another lethal female whose gun is clearly her only fashion accessory!

CHAPTER SIX

FRONTIER FLOOZIES

I don't envy those Western regulars with all that action, the shooting, riding, roping, and falling. I never made another.

—Hedy Lamarr (following the release of *Copper Canyon*)

HE Western is probably the most identifiable, durable, and beloved staple of American moviemaking. These sagas usually unfolded from a distinctly male point of view, with the emphasis on the hero (typically in a white hat), the villain, and the epic struggle of good vs. evil. This was a most simplistic formula: movies made by men, about men, for men; with the lawman and his black-garbed nemesis (subtle, weren't they?) generating most of the attention. This highly stylized account of frontier days, sold to the rest of the world as the quintessential standard of the Old West, seldom veered from it. Into this patriarchy rides the distaff. These sagebrush sinners now received the same screen time afforded to their acting brethren. There were a few bad girl sightings on the range as far back as 1926, when the beautiful Nita Cavaleri turned the tables on her costar Bob Custer (and pulled a pistol on him to boot) in *The Dead-line*. Producers were quick to get the hint that fallen women, tempting a buckaroo (temporarily of course) before he rode off into the sunset, introduced a sex appeal these pictures had never had before.

However, not everything was glamorous for our assorted dance hall dames on the 1930s and 1940s Western sets. The locations were tough, the conditions uncomfortable, and due to budget restrictions, actresses often did their own hair and makeup. There was also the stigma of being labeled a Western starlet, which meant they weren't even considered for other roles. Gradually things began to change when top box-office stars such as Ann Sheridan, Kay Francis, and Jennifer Jones climbed onto the buckboard, making it not only acceptable to appear in a horse opera but fashionable too. Others like Claire Trevor, Maureen O'Hara, and Barbara Stanwyck were right at home on horseback. The earthy sexual energy they brought to the genre not only kept the censors busy (Jane Russell's debut in *The Outlaw* was nothing short of scandalous) but helped usher in a newfound popularity for the dime store cowboy novel, now with a more defined lustiness. No wholesome schoolmarms in this group; these ladies put the bawdy in bawdyhouse. So from Marlene Dietrich to Raquel Welch we round up a posse of the roughest, toughest fillies this side of Amarillo.

Ready to saddle up?

A wanted criminal (Anthony Quinn) finds time for a little diversion in the form of a fiery (was there any other kind?) Mexican peasant girl named Elena, played by Lita Milan (1933–), in *The Ride Back* (United Artists, 1957). It was another wildcat role for the former cover-girl-turned-starlet.

The Furies (Paramount, 1950) was a brilliant and sometimes disturbing Western directed by Anthony Mann, a legend in this genre. Barbara Stanwyck (1907–90) played the slightly unbalanced daughter of a cattle rancher, Walter Huston (glimpsed in the mirror with Judith Anderson), in his last motion picture. This moody, rather adult saga received an Academy Award nomination for cinematography. (JC Archives)

SCENE STILL

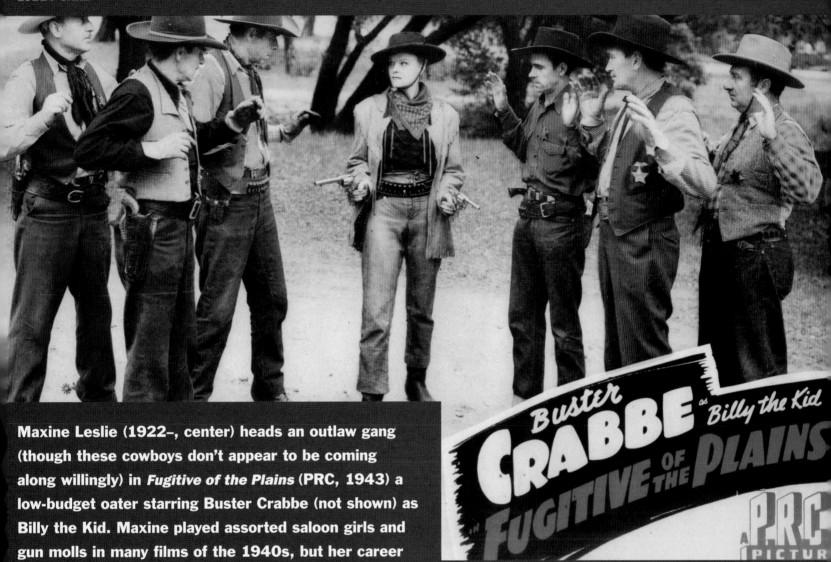

Maxine Leslie (1922–, center) heads an outlaw gang (though these cowboys don't appear to be coming along willingly) in *Fugitive of the Plains* (PRC, 1943) a low-budget oater starring Buster Crabbe (not shown) as Billy the Kid. Maxine played assorted saloon girls and gun molls in many films of the 1940s, but her career stalled shortly thereafter.

Vivacious, leggy redhead Tracey Roberts (1914–2002) was an unforgettable dance hall hostess and the only female distraction in *Fort Defiance* (United Artists, 1951), a minor Western and one of the scores of films and television shows that Tracey, a Broadway veteran, made during her long career. Tracey later became a top acting coach and repertory theater director.

Truly one of the best of the worst, *Apache Woman* (American Releasing Corp., 1955) starred Joan Taylor (1929–) in the title role as a tempestuous half-breed who falls for a government agent (Lloyd Bridges) assigned to bridge a gap between her people and the U.S. military. Joan stepped into another pair of moccasins two years later for *War Drums* (1957) as — you guessed it — an Indian hellcat!

Myrna Dell (1924–) plays the cold-blooded daughter of a wealthy land baron and makes an aggressive withdrawal from an equally ruthless banker (Charles Trowbridge) in *The Bushwhackers* (Realart, 1952) before losing her life in the transaction. Myrna made nearly sixty films (of varying quality) but was always at her best when cast as grasping harpies. (JC Archives)

SCENE STILL

LOBBY CARD

A greedy claim jumper, Ida Lupino (1914–95), stops at nothing to protect her interests in a gold mine in the prophetically titled *Lust for Gold* (Columbia, 1949). Here Ida stands guard at the entrance to the quarry with costar William Prince. After an impressive film career that began in her native England in 1932 and included some seventy motion pictures, Ida tried her luck behind the camera and became a highly regarded producer and director.

As incredulous as it sounds, Marlene Dietrich (1901–92) was considered "washed-up" by theater exhibitors nationwide just prior to the release of *Destry Rides Again* (Universal, 1939), a rollicking Western classic. The huge success of the film put the Teutonic siren back on the celluloid map. In this scene Marlene, as sassy saloon singer Frenchie, prepares to square off with town busybody Una Merkel (1903–86, one of Hollywood's most in-demand character actresses) in a legendary movie catfight. Remade in 1950 with Shelley Winters and again in 1954 with Mari Blanchard, this 1939 version is still the champ. (JC Archives)

A mud-splattered Peggie Castle (1926–73) means business as the pistol-toting Marie "Oklahoma" Saunders in *The Oklahoma Woman* (A.I.P., 1956). Peggie played the cold-blooded outlaw queen who controls a corrupt Western town in this low-budget adventure yam, one of the many she starred in during the 1950s. Peggie left show business after appearing as a saloon owner on the television series *The Lawman* from 1959 to 1962. (JC Archives)

Lanky Rod Cameron (left) and his gang try to subdue Ruth Roman (1922–99) as the feisty *Belle Starr's Daughter* (Fox, 1948) who is hell-bent on revenge for her mother's murder. Ruth paid her dues in dozens of bit parts over the years as native girls and hand-maidens before producers recognized her potential for so much more. *Belle Starr's Daughter* was one of Ruth's first starring roles, and though it's only a fair Western, her performance doesn't disappoint.

Julie Latour, a bewitching saloon singer played by Vera Ralston (1919–2003), is desired by several men (naturally) in *Jubilee Trail* (Republic, 1954). Vera, seen here with costars Barton MacLane (left) and Jim Davis (right), was a champion ice-skater in her native Czechoslovakia and was originally signed by Republic Pictures to duplicate the success of Sonja Henie in a string of minor musicals, but studio chief Herbert J. Yates was so enamored with her that he spared no expense in a failed attempt to make her a top dramatic star. Interestingly, no other Hollywood producer ever sought to use Vera's services and all of her twenty-six films were made under the watchful eye of Yates, who eventually married Vera in 1952. She retired six years later.

The talented Joanne Dru (1922–96) starred in two classic American Westerns, *Red River* and *She Wore a Yellow Ribbon*, in 1948 and 1949, respectively. After such an auspicious start, the low-budget *Outlaw Territory* (Realart, 1953) was quite a comedown for the young star. As saloon hostess Hannah Lee (the original title), Joanne attracts the carnal attentions of a hired killer (Macdonald Carey), even though she really loves someone else. This cheaply-made adventure was originally filmed in 3-D.

Western vengeance, bad girl style with Raquel Welch (1940–) in *Bandelero!* (Fox, 1968), a spirited adventure highlighted by some wonderful location photography and an energetic performance by the gorgeous Raquel, seen here gaining an obvious advantage over an outlaw gang. Raquel saddled up again for *100 Rifles*, also in 1968, and as *Hannie Caulder* in 1971.

LOBBY CARD

For the first five years of her movie career, Linda Darnell (1921–65) was typecast as sweet, virtuous young ladies, but things changed for the *badder* when Fox wisely cast the stunning brunette in more aggressive, sexually charged roles (*Hangover Square*, *My Darling Clementine*, *Forever Amber*, and *A Letter to Three Wives* are among her best) that suited her perfectly. *Black Spurs* (Paramount, 1965) was Linda's final film. Once again she played a gaudy saloon hostess, this time with Lon Chaney Jr. (center) and Rory Calhoun (right). This dreadfully cheap Western was released after Linda's tragic death in a house fire while on tour in a play.

LOBBY CARD

Don't let that dainty bonnet fool you; Penny Edwards (1928–98) means business as the head of a band of female outlaws in *The Dalton Girls* (United Artists, 1957). Here Penny gets the drop on costar John Russell in this low-budget Western, one of many that Penny made over a ten-year period. Penny's fellow gang members were Merry Anders, Lisa Davis, and Sue George.

THE DALTON GIRLS

starring MERRY LISA PENNY SUE JOHN
ANDERS · DAVIS · EDWARDS · GEORGE · RUSSELL · Screenplay by MAURICE TOMBRAGEL · Music by BAXTER · Directed by REGINALD LE BORG · HOWARD W. KOCH · Produced by AUBREY SCHENCK · A BEL-AIR Production · RELEASED THRU UNITED ARTISTS

A U.S. marshal (George Montgomery, right) and his deputy (Tab Hunter, left) square off over a fetching dance hall gal who is being transported to prison for murder in *Hostile Guns* (Paramount, 1967). Yvonne De Carlo (1922–) played the convicted murderess who was romantically involved with Montgomery years before, which complicates their already hazardous journey.

Aviation billionaire and movie-studio mogul Howard Hughes directed the cult Western *The Outlaw* (RKO, 1941) and was therefore able to dote on the film's star (and Hughes protégée) Jane Russell (1921–). Though *The Outlaw* contained a solid performance by Walter Huston as Doc Holliday, it was Jane's cleavage — or rather the amount of it displayed — that garnered all the publicity. Rumors of a longer, uncensored version were never proven and Jane's career continued quite nicely for many years.

A U.S. officer (John Payne, pictured) pledges to keep construction of the railroad running smoothly in *Rails Into Laramie* (Universal, 1954), but he meets opposition from the local bad guy and a cheap dance hall hostess played by Mari Blanchard (1927–70), who later becomes his ally. Mari, an ex-model, was right at home in these colorful adventures and was usually found entertaining the boys in gaudy saloon settings throughout the 1950s.

SCENE STILL

How about this one: A Western filmed in Spain with a British crew! The picture was *The Sheriff of Fractured Jaw* (Fox, 1958) and the result is so much better than the budget (or the title) implies. Jayne Mansfield (1932–67) is delightful as a tough saloon owner who has the whole town in her control.

Sophia Loren (1934–) appeared in a variety of films in her long career, but *Heller in Pink Tights* (Paramount, 1960) was her only Western. A blonde Sophia was an eyeful as a much desired member of a traveling theatrical troupe touring the Old West. Despite being a first-rate production (directed by George Cukor), the critical response was less than enthusiastic.

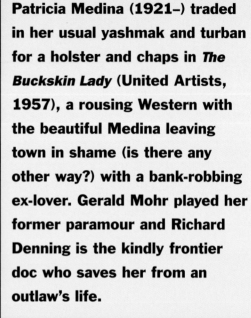

Patricia Medina (1921–) traded in her usual yashmak and turban for a holster and chaps in *The Buckskin Lady* (United Artists, 1957), a rousing Western with the beautiful Medina leaving town in shame (is there any other way?) with a bank-robbing ex-lover. Gerald Mohr played her former paramour and Richard Denning is the kindly frontier doc who saves her from an outlaw's life.

Can Hopalong Cassidy (William Boyd) resist the obvious charms of a cantina dancer with smolder to spare? In *The Eagle's Brood* (Paramount, 1935) Hoppy's life is saved by a famous desperado, so he agrees to find the outlaw's missing son, which eventually leads him to the vampish Dolores, played by Joan Woodbury (1915–89). Joan worked originally under her real name, Nana Martinez, before changing it to something less ethnic, which extended her Hollywood career another thirty years. (JC Archives)

20th CENTURY-FOX presents

THE RIVER'S EDGE

BENEDICT BOGEAUS
PRODUCTION

COLOR by DE LUXE
CINEMASCOPE

PRODUCED BY **BENEDICT BOGEAUS** DIRECTED BY **ALLAN DWAN**

SCREEN PLAY BY **HAROLD JACOB SMITH** AND **JAMES LEICESTER**

STARRING
RAY MILLAND · ANTHONY QUINN · DEBRA PAGET

BASED ON A STORY
"THE HIGHEST MOUNTAIN"
BY HAROLD JACOB SMITH

LOBBY CARD

A money-hungry trio plans to cross the Mexican border with a suitcase full of loot in
The River's Edge (Fox, 1957), a searing contemporary Western. Ray Milland (right) and
Anthony Quinn (left) are adversaries and uneasy partners, and Debra Paget (1933–), as
Milland's ex-flame and Quinn's current wife, is the babe (of course) who exasperates the
already sticky situation.

James Stewart and Henry Fonda find themselves running a Wyoming bordello in the raucous Western comedy *The Cheyenne Social Club* (NGP, 1970), co-starring the voluptuous Sue Ane Langdon (1936–) as Opal Ann, a bawdy-house girl. Sue Ane (second from the left) was a sexy, bubbly (and sometimes blonde) comic actress who added a unique brand of daffy fun to a long list of films and television programs. Sue Ane's fellow working girls are (from left) Elaine Devry (1932–), Jackie Russell (1939–, rear), Jackie Joseph (1934–), and Sharon DeBord (1939–). (JC Archives)

Western movie hero Richard Martin investigates a smuggling ring that's running guns across the Mexican border with the help of a bevy of shapely saloon tarts headed by Cleo Moore (1928–73) in *Rio Grande Patrol* (RKO, 1950). Cleo played Peppie who is causing some difficulties in this scene for the ever valiant guy in the white hat. (JC Archives)

A moral-minded (yet sinister) sheriff (John Pickard, right) has all the loose women run out of his town in *The Black Whip* (Regal, 1956), a modest co-feature starring Adele Mara (1923–, left) and Coleen Gray (1922–, center) as two of the trollops who are helped by renegade members of Quantrell's Raiders. Both Adele and Coleen appeared in dozens of Westerns (among many other films) during their careers and had long runs in the genre. (JC Archives)

SCENE STILL

Albert Dekker (left) played real-life lawman Bat Masterson who is torn between his job and a flashy dance hall dame played by Claire Trevor (1909–2000) in *Woman of the Town* (United Artists, 1943). This was a standard bit of casting for Claire, who was at the peak of her professional popularity. At the right is actor Barry Sullivan, who made his feature film debut in this entertaining Western.

LOBBY CARD

SCENE STILL

Greed and double-crossing get the better of a motley group of characters in *The Tall Texan* (Lippert, 1953) during a search for gold at an ancient Indian burial ground. Marie Windsor (1919–2000), seen here with Lloyd Bridges, worked harder than was necessary in this grade-B oater, but her performances were certainly never dull! (JC Archives)

Beverly Garland (1926–, with gun) is known as *The Gunslinger* (A.I.P., 1956) when she becomes the sheriff of a lawless community after the marshal — her husband — is killed. It appears she is not making much of an impression on the vicious town madam, played with great relish by Allison Hayes (1930–77). Allison is considered one of the great movie bad girls by film buffs, a screen persona she utilized in more than twenty Bs, including *The Attack of the 50 Ft. Woman*, a masterpiece of awful filmmaking. (JC Archives)

SCENE STILL

They just don't get any cornier than *The Singing Sheriff* (Universal, 1944) a pastiche of Western action, comedy, and music, starring Iris Adrian (1913–94) as Lefty, a hard-bitten honky-tonk gal involved with a gang of desperados. Rubber-faced comic Fuzzy Knight (pictured with Iris) provided the slapstick and Iris supplied the wisecracks, both to perfection. (JC Archives)

PORTRAIT STILL

In a change-of-pace role for this Oscar-winning actress Jennifer Jones (1919–) transformed herself into the copper-skinned half-caste Pearl Chavez in the grand epic Western *Duel in the Sun* (Selznick Releasing, 1946), based on the novel by Niven Busch. Perhaps the critics didn't buy Jennifer as a degenerate temptress, but audiences did, and the picture (with its frank sensual tone) succeeded, at least financially, earning Jennifer another Academy Award nomination (her fourth of five) for her work. (JC Archives)

The combination of Betty Grable (1916–73), the queen of the flashy Hollywood musical, and Preston Sturges, a premier film director, would seem like a surefire hit, but their joint effort, *The Beautiful Blonde from Bashful Bend* (Fox, 1949), was a huge box-office dud. Time has been kinder to this movie than critics were in 1949, and it does offer a glimpse of a slightly *badder* Betty (center) as saloon girl Freddie Jones, who was quite handy with a six-shooter. Joining the hijinks are (from left) Olga San Juan (1927–, as Betty's partner on the lam), Rudy Vallee, Sterling Holloway, and Danny Jackson. (JC Archives)

Kathleen Hughes (1928–) strikes a very welcoming pose as a typical painted-up hussy in *Dawn at Socorro* (Universal, 1954), a predictable Western that had her working for gambling house owner David Brian. Kathleen, who appeared in several fondly remembered sci-fi flicks of the 1950s, was at her nastiest the year before as a blackmailing starlet in *The Glass Web*. (JC Archives)

CHAPTER SEVEN

MAKE MINE MINK

If you want to see the girl next door, go next door.
—Joan Crawford

FUNNY bad girl? Bad girls in comedies? As contradictory as the term may seem, these characters have been a staple in Hollywood films since the 1920s. When played for laughs or presented in a light-hearted way, the bad girl appeared less threatening and perhaps a bit more three-dimensional as a result. Comically speaking, she might seem a tad more developed, pun intended!

Surely Mae West, Carole Lombard, and Jean Harlow were Depression-era favorites, and they naughtily took a poke at the ongoing battle of the sexes and drove the censors a little crazy. Tinseltown toughies like Joan Blondell, Una Merkel, Wynne Gibson, and Marion Martin made gold digging more acceptable by adding a hefty dose of humor. The public adored these sexually liberated women who could toss off their ermine wrap as easily as they could a stinging *bon mot*.

Later Judy Holliday perfected the role of the scatterbrained gun moll in *Born Yesterday* and won an Oscar for it. By the mid-1950s Marilyn Monroe played the quintessential dizzy fortune hunter in several classic comedies, which were made even more special with her unique blend of vulnerability and dead-on comic timing. Most of her imitators (and there were many) could never make such a claim. Later in the decade and in the 1960s we saw Shirley MacLaine add her unforgettable touch to a string of good-hearted hookers (*Some Came Running, Irma la Douce,* etc.) with plenty of cockeyed optimism. Since then actresses as diverse as Madeline Kahn, Jamie Lee Curtis, and Barbra Streisand have put their stamp on variations of the wise-cracking prostitute with a heart of gold. The genre was given a major boost in 1990 with the very successful *Pretty Woman* with Julia Roberts as a sentimental streetwalker. However, by then the notion of a delightful doxy seemed somewhat dated. Let's face it, happy hookers just ain't what they used to be!

In *Value for Money* (Rank, 1955) young Yorkshire chap (John Gregson) inherits a windfall and sets off for London to start spending it. Diana Dors (1931–84) played the gold digger who has no trouble helping him dispose of his newly found wealth. This was a typical bit of casting for Diana at the time, who was dubbed "the hurricane in mink" by the British press.

GEORGE
GoBel
MITZI
GAYNOR
DAVID
NIVEN

IN

THE BIRDS AND THE BEES

Color by
Technicolor

Co-starring
REGINALD **GARDINER** · FRED **CLARK**

Produced by Paul Jones · Directed by Norman Taurog
Screen Play by Sidney Sheldon and Preston Sturges

Based on a Story by Monckton Hoffe · Musical Numbers Staged by Nick Castle · New Songs by Harry Warren and Mack David

A Paramount Picture

A hapless George Gobel gets an earful from a pretty card shark played by Mitzi Gaynor (1930–) in *The Birds and the Bees* (Paramount, 1956), a rather uninspired remake of the classic 1941 comedy *The Lady Eve*, with Mitzi turning in a fine comedic performance in a role originated by Barbara Stanwyck.

Natalie Wood (1938–81) had the title role as *Penelope* (MGM, 1966), a lackluster comedy concerning a neglected wife who plots to rob her own husband's bank in a silly attempt to gain his attention. Ian Bannen portrayed her spouse in this career misfire for Natalie, who had been a working actress from the age of five.

Edie Adams (1927–) has done it all: Broadway, nightclubs, television, commercials, and recordings. The former Miss New York TV and Juilliard graduate also brightened a number of films in the 1960s including *Lover Come Back* (Universal, 1961), the second of three Doris Day/Rock Hudson comedies. Edie played the ambitious showgirl Rebel Davis who plans to testify against unethical adman Hudson (pictured) until he makes her a TV spokeswoman for a nonexistent product called Vip. Edie was married to comedian Ernie Kovacs from 1955 until his death in 1962.

155

The slightly amusing comedy *She Wouldn't Say Yes* (Columbia, 1945) was designed as a vehicle for Rosalind Russell. However, the picture was stolen by a sassy blonde named Adele Jergens (1917–2002), seen here with a very perplexed Lee Bowman. Adele, a former beauty contestant winner and chorus girl, decorated many second features in the 1940s and 1950s, usually as a tart-tongued showgirl or a racketeer's girl-friend. She is most famous for playing Marilyn Monroe's mother (though in reality she was only nine years older than Marilyn) in *Ladies of the Chorus*, a grade-B musical about a mother/daughter burlesque team.

COLUMBIA PICTURES presents
Rosalind *Lee*
RUSSELL · BOWMAN
in
She Wouldn't Say Yes

e's got him helpless . . . and **you** helpless with laughter!

LOBBY CARD

SCENE STILL

After leaving her native Montreal, Fifi D'Orsay (1904–83) became a vaudeville headliner before enter-ing films in 1929. Fifi was frequently cast as a pouting Parisian fortune hunter with a comically thick French accent. In one of her early starring roles in *The Girl From Calgary* (Monogram, 1932), Fifi tries to break up a fight between two suitors, Paul Kelly (center) and Robert Warwick (right), who are vying for her affections. (JC Archives)

Gorgeous Jill St. John (1940–) finds husband-hunting to be a rather dangerous sport in *Honeymoon Hotel* (MGM, 1964) as the tipsy Jill is reprimanded by an angry charwoman played with great zeal by the wonderful Elsa Lanchester. It appears, however, that Jill's found Mr. Right (Robert Goulet) in this frothy comedy. Jill played some kooky mantraps in numerous films but none were terribly memorable. Her best performance is as the ravishing jewel smuggler Tiffany Case in the Bond adventure *Diamonds Are Forever*, but it was one of her last major motion pictures. The still-stunning actress is now Mrs. Robert Wagner.

Constance Bennett (1904–65) had the kind of glamorous life that could have easily served as the plot for one of her many movies. Her screen debut in 1921 launched her into the spotlight, and as her fame grew she became a glittering member of the international smart-set. Connie (as she was referred to by the press) played elegant (if slightly hard), imperious, worldly playthings in films with titles that could represent chapters from her own life: *Reckless Youth*, *Married*, *Rich People*, *Sin Takes a Holiday*, *Lady With a Past*, *Bed of Roses*, *Service De Luxe*, *Sin Town*, and *Smart Woman*. She was eclipsed in popularity by her younger sister Joan who came on the scene a few years later and worked in more dramatically diverse motion pictures.

If you think it looks like petty thief Mickey Rooney would do just about anything for a fortune-hunting redhead, played by Elaine Stewart (1929–), in *A Slight Case of Larceny* (MGM, 1953), you would be right. Elaine appeared in some important films during her contract with Metro in the 1950s, including a memorable role as an ambitious starlet in *The Bad and the Beautiful* the previous year.

A gullible officer, played by James Booth (seen here with British character actor Lionel Jeffries), is tricked by a trio of predatory females, including a sexy murderess, played by Stella Stevens (1936–), in *The Secret of My Success* (MGM, 1965). An underrated actress and comedienne, Stella wasn't given much to do in films aside from just looking great, which she certainly accomplished. She does turn in a heartbreaking performance as a prostitute in *The Ballad of Cable Hogue* in 1970 and later worked primarily on television appearing in more than twenty-five made-for-TV movies.

Broderick Crawford and Claire Trevor (1909–2000) mug it up in *Stop, You're Killing Me* (Warner Bros., 1952), a lightweight comedy about a gangster and his gal who are trying to go legit. This was familiar territory for Claire, who spent the better part of her career playing floozies and shady ladies in scores of films beginning in 1933. She won a Best Supporting Actress Oscar for her role as an alcoholic gun moll in *Key Largo* in 1948.

PORTRAIT CARD

A WARNER BROS. RIOT!

DAMON RUNYON'S "Stop, You're Killing Me"

WARNERCOLOR

BRODERICK CRAWFORD · CLAIRE TREVOR

It would be nearly impossible to steal a scene from Julie Andrews, but in *Victor/Victoria* (MGM/UA, 1982) Lesley Ann Warren (1946–) did just that. In the chic, sophisticated, gender-bending comedy directed by Blake Edwards, Lesley Ann was the hilariously coarse Norma Cassidy, a gangster's gal, visiting the very gay Paree. Lesley Ann was nominated for a Best Supporting Actress Academy Award and a Golden Globe for her memorable performance. (JC Archives)

Leggy Sheree North (1933–) collects her diploma (and the admiration of the male students) in *How to Be Very, Very Popular* (Fox, 1955), a wafer-thin comedy about two dancers (Betty Grable was the other) who try to elude gangsters by pretending to be college girls. Presumably Marilyn Monroe wisely turned down the film and Sheree, a studio contract player, was the next choice. A professional hoofer in her teens, Sheree has appeared in hundreds of movies and television roles usually as down-on-their-luck dames. Sheree, who's worked with everyone from Elvis to Seinfeld, developed into one of Hollywood's most respected character actresses and has even taught several drama classes.

Debonair butler David Niven tends to willful heiress Martha Hyer (1924–) in *My Man Godfrey* (Universal, 1957), a rather pale remake of the 1936 original. Since 1946 Martha has graced countless films in which she was usually cast as a spoiled, self-centered society girl. She was nominated once for an Oscar for her performance in *Some Came Running* in 1959.

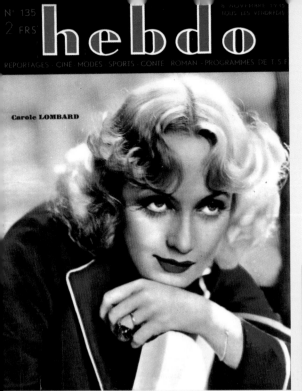

N° 135
2 FRS

REPORTAGES · CINE · MODES · SPORTS · CONTE · ROMAN · PROGRAMMES DE T.S.F

hebdo

Carole LOMBARD

FOREIGN MAGAZINE

Carole Lombard (1908–42) is the beautiful cover subject of *Hebdo* (France, November 1935). Carole made more than two dozen Mack Sennett slapstick shorts in the 1920s in which she perfected her precise comic timing. Before her emergence as a brilliant comedienne Carole played routine tough-blondes (*Sinners in the Sun, No Man of Her Own,* etc.) before her big break in the classic screwball comedy *Twentieth Century* (1934). At the height of her fame she was killed in a plane crash while touring the country on behalf of the war effort, leaving an inconsolable Clark Gable (they wed in 1939) a widower.

Here is the winsome yet wicked Leslie Brooks (1922–) in a publicity picture from the comedy *The Corpse Came C.O.D.* (Columbia, 1947), based on the James Starr pulp novel. It was just one of the countless Bs Leslie appeared in during the 1940s, most often in bitchy "other woman" roles. She was at her most venomous in the independent cheapie *Blonde Ice* (Film Classics, 1948) which was sadly also one of her last films. (JC Archives)

PORTRAIT STILL

Statuesque blonde bombshell Joi Lansing (1928–72) played glamorous bit parts in many films of the late-1940s and 1950s, often uncredited. Can you spot her in *Easter Parade, Take Me Out to the Ball Game,* and *Singin' in the Rain*? Oddly two of Joi's starring vehicles (both as gang molls) were in the similarly titled *Hot Cars* and *Hot Shots,* both released within a few months of each other in 1956. It was television that gave Joi better opportunities, first on *The Bob Cummings Show* and later on *The Beverly Hillbillies.* (JC Archives)

PUBLICITY STILL

Joyce Compton (1907–97) played feather-brained floozies in nearly two hundred features and comedy shorts beginning in 1925, and for more than thirty years she supplied comic support to practically every major film star working in Hollywood. In *Sing, Sinner, Sing* (Majestic Pictures, 1933) Joyce is a nightclub hostess who sets her sights on playboy Donald Dillaway. The film was rereleased under the more succinct title *Clip Joint*. Joyce left pictures in 1958 and became a nurse. (JC Archives)

Cinemonde (France, December 1959) offers up a wholesome holiday cover of Mamie Van Doren (1932–), who was probably on more than one Christmas wish list that year! Mamie, a former band singer, became one of the many platinum bombshells during the 1950s who tried to give Marilyn Monroe a run for the money, but her films (who can forget *The Beautiful Legs of Sabrina* and *Born Reckless*, to name just two) rarely rose above the exploitative.

FOREIGN MAGAZINE

Jean Harlow (1911–37), Hollywood's original platinum blonde, had already appeared in more than a dozen films and comedy shorts when Howard Hughes tapped her for his aviation melodrama *Hell's Angels* in 1930, but critics were initially unkind towards the budding starlet. It wasn't until Jean signed with MGM a couple of years later, when the studio wisely focused on her natural flair for comedy (and played up her delightfully coarse brassiness), that Jean's career kicked into high gear. The public responded by making Jean a top box-office attraction. Among her best are *Red Dust*, *Hold Your Man*, *Bombshell*, *Dinner at Eight*, and *Libeled Lady*. While filming *Saratoga* with Clark Gable, she died of uremic poisoning at the age of twenty-six.

CIGARETTE CARD

Mae West (1892–1980) took Hollywood by storm in 1932 after great success in vaude-ville and on Broadway, where she wrote, produced, and directed her first play entitled *Sex*. It was ruled obscene (it was, after all, 1926), and Mae spent ten days in jail because of it. She conquered film next and kept the censors on their toes with saucy dialogue (which she usually wrote herself) laced with clever double-entendres. Her movies single-handedly saved Paramount Pictures from the brink of bankruptcy during the 1930s. By the end of the decade, she was running out of steam and wisely turned her attention back to the theater with a risqué revue, *Catherine Was Great.* A widely publicized return to motion pictures, at the age of seventy-eight, in *Myra Breckenridge* (1970) proved that she still had the magic even though the film was a disaster. The legendary bad girl once growled, "It's better to be looked over than overlooked." (It is doubtful she ever had such a problem.)

CIGARETTE CARD

ARCADE CARD

The always suave Adolphe Menjou is suspicious of cynical gold digger Joan Blondell (1909–79) and her interest in bumbling businessman Guy Kibbee in *Convention City* (First National, 1933), an amusing programmer. Joan was one of the busiest actresses in Hollywood and worked on as many as ten films in one year alone. She made an easy transition to character parts by the early 1950s, appeared in more than one hundred motion pictures, and received an Oscar nomination for her role in *The Blue Veil* in 1951.

FOREIGN MAGAZINE

Über sex-symbol Jayne Mansfield (1932–67) strikes an inviting pose on an issue of *Cinemonde* (France, July 1963). Jayne was one of filmdom's brightest lights during the sexually repressed Eisenhower 1950s, making an indelible impression in Fox comedies (she was a dizzy gangster's girlfriend in *The Girl Can't Help It* in 1956, among others), in which she perfected the dumb-blond stereotype and made it uniquely her own. Her career faltered some in the following decade, and she found herself resorting to self-parody in a string of virtually unwatchable continental clinkers. Jayne was killed in a car accident en route to a nightclub engagement in 1967.

LOBBY CARD

Machine Gun Mama (PRC, 1944) was a zany poverty row quickie which starred Sonora-born starlet Armida (1911–89) as the tough-talking owner of a traveling carnival overrun with gangsters. Armida began playing hot-blooded, castenet-clicking señoritas (usually with names like Rosita, Lolita, Pepita, or Conchita) in a string of no-budget adventure films in her native Mexico.

PRC Pictures presents
armida
MACHINE GUN MAMA

ONE SHEET POSTER

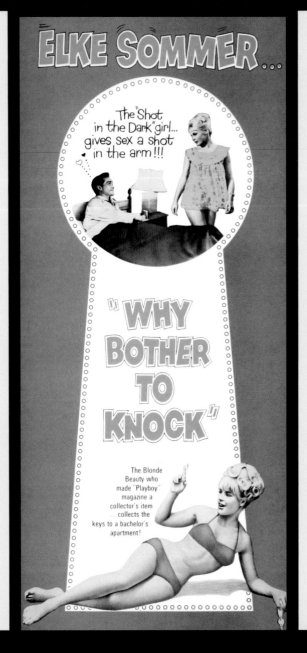

INSERT POSTER

The Most Wanted Man (Astor, 1960 rerelease) provided Zsa Zsa Gabor (1917–) with one of her best roles, and she delivers a memorable comic performance. In the film (originally made in France in 1953 under the title *Public Enemy Number One*) Zsa Zsa is Lola, a gorgeous lady gangster who sets her trap for the bumbling Fernandel, one of France's most beloved funnymen.

A headstrong young fräulein, played by Elke Sommer (1940–), turns the tables on a swinging bachelor in the pedestrian comedy *Why Bother to Knock* (Seven Arts, 1961), costarring Richard Todd. The film was released again three years later to coincide with Elke's sexy photo layout in Playboy and her success in the motion picture *A Shot in the Dark*. Elke has been scorching the screen internationally since 1958, when the German-born starlet made her film debut in *This Angry Age*. She has worked consistently ever since in nearly one hundred movies and is also an accomplished painter.

SCENE STILL

Gildersleeve's Ghost (RKO, 1944) was another entry in the popular series of screen comedies starring Harold Peary as Throckmorton P. Gildersleeve. This time a horror twist was added to the silliness as Gildy tangles with a mad scientist (Frank Reicher, center) and his henchman (Joseph Vitale, right). Further complicating things is a smart-alecky chorus girl (who can become invisible!) played by Marion Martin (1908–85). Though Marion played pushy gold diggers in scores of films, she was actually born into East Coast society and only considered a show biz career when her family was financially destroyed in the stock market crash of 1929. (JC Archives)

When it came to dizzy comic relief, nobody supplied it with more gusto than the prolific Joyce Jameson (1932–87), one of Hollywood's favorite dumb blondes. Joyce made her debut as a chorus girl in the musical film *Show Boat* (1951) and racked up more than eighty TV and movie roles during her career. Here Joyce spices up a scene from *The Split* (MGM, 1968), a routine heist film costarring tough guy Warren Oates. (JC Archives)

SCENE STILL

WINDOW CARD

Raquel Welch (1940–) displays a wonderful comic ability (and apparently so much more) in *The Biggest Bundle of Them All* (MGM, 1968), which was filmed internationally with an all-star cast. In it Raquel is a sexy member of a bumbling criminal gang that plans to kidnap an American mobster.

Hollywood's favorite villainess Gale Sondergaard (1899–1985) was a theater-trained actress who won the very first Oscar for a supporting actress for her film debut in *Anthony Adverse*. Largely wasted in mediocre material, Gale sometimes resorted to parodying her own menacing screen persona in films like *My Favorite Spy* (Paramount, 1942) with Bob Hope. Unfairly blacklisted by the House Un-American Activities Committee she was tragically denied movie roles for twenty years. (JC Archives)

Iris Adrian (1913–94), the film industry's most reliable comic character actress, added a tough, brassy spark to more than 130 motion pictures and countless television shows for more than fifty years. This extremely rare scene of Iris (as wisecracking carnival dancer Toots O'Day) and Fuzzy Knight from *New York Town* (Paramount, 1941) was cut from the final release print. (JC Archives)

In films for just fourteen years, Wynne Gibson (1903–87) racked up an impressive resume filled with a roster of gold diggers and fallen women. In *Lady and Gent* (Paramount, 1932) Wynne was a cheap speakeasy hostess named Puff Rogers who falls hard for a broken-down prizefighter (George Bancroft). Her final feature was *Mystery Broadcast* in 1943, after which she became a top Hollywood talent agent. (JC Archives)

SCENE STILL

Few actresses could imbue what were essentially stereotypical characters with so much humor and depth as Barbara Nichols (1929–76) who appeared in several wonderful films in the 1950s and 1960s, including the screen version of *The Pajama Game* (Warner Bros., 1957), directed by George Abbott and Stanley Donen. As Poopsie, an employee of the Sleeptite Pajama Company, Barbara (seen here with Eddie Foy Jr. and Carol Haney, who was also in the original Broadway production) quite typically walks away with every scene she's in. (JC Archives)

SCENE STILL

METRO-GOLDWYN-MAYER PRESENTS

A MARTIN MELCHER-EVERETT FREEMAN PRODUCTION

STARRING

DORIS DAY
ROD TAYLOR
ARTHUR GODFREY

The Glass Bottom Boat

CO-STARRING

JOHN McGIVER · PAUL LYNDE · EDWARD ANDREWS · ERIC FLEMING · DOM DE LUISE
AND DICK MARTIN · WRITTEN BY EVERETT FREEMAN · DIRECTED BY FRANK TASHLIN · PRODUCED BY MARTIN MELCHER AND EVERETT FREEMAN

PRESS BOOK DETAIL

Doris Day (1924–) a bad girl? Well, technically no, though the multitalented legend did have a bit of fun with her wholesome image in a dream sequence contained within the Frank Tashlin comedy *The Glass Bottom Boat* (MGM, 1966). Suspecting her of being a spy, costar Rod Taylor visualizes Doris as a seductive Mata Hari, complete with a beaded headdress and a strategically placed jewel in her navel.

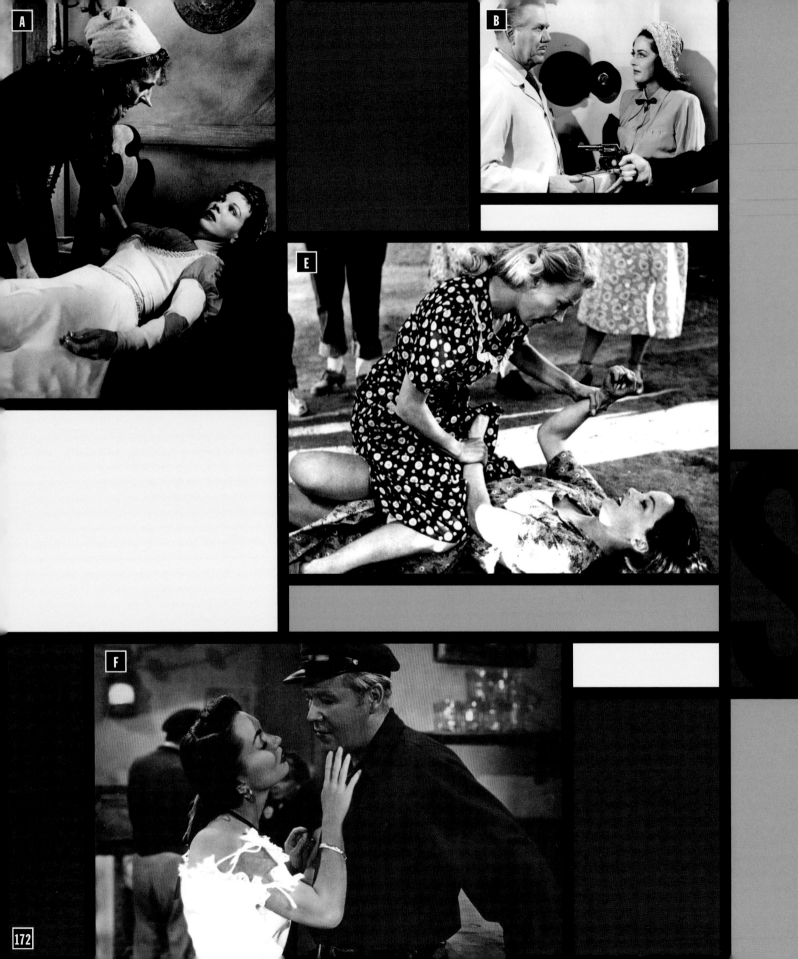

INDEX

I

"HELL BOUND"

ARCADE CARD: 5 x 8 inches and smaller. These charming (and inexpensively produced) postcards were printed in full color, sepia tone, and black and white on heavier card stock and were sold in penny arcade vending machines. Others could be obtained by simply sending a fan letter to your favorite star (also called a FAN or PHOTO CARD).

CIGARETTE CARD: Roughly 2 x 2 inches. These postcards were printed in full color, sepia tone, and black and white on heavier card stock and were sold in cigarette packs. See also ARCADE CARD.

FOREIGN MAGAZINE: Approximately 11 x 15 inches, though sizes varied. Featuring full color, sepia toned, or black and white covers, the publications were rarely distributed in the United States and offer a fascinating glimpse into the history of international publicity.

HALF SHEET POSTER: 22 x 28 inches, typically printed on paper (similar to inserts). This flat art often featured different images than those that appeared on one sheets.

INSERT: 11 x 36 inches, typically printed on card stock (similar to half sheet posters). This flat art often featured different images than those that appeared on one sheets.

LOBBY CARD: 11 x 14 inches, full color and duotone, printed on card stock and distributed in sets of eight. They depicted films scenes and hung in movie theater lobbies.

ONE SHEET POSTER: 27 x 41 inches, full color and duotone. They are the most prized among collectors due to their size. Prior to 1985, studios folded one sheets — sometimes in the smaller 11 x 14 size — and distributed them in round film canisters for unique promotional packaging.

PORTRAIT CARD: 11 x 14 inches. Sometimes found in a lobby card set, the portrait card did not feature a scene from the film but rather a highly stylized, studio-engineered image, typically of the movie's stars.

PORTRAIT STILL: 8 x 10 inches, glossy black and white or color. Used for general publicity of a particular actress, though not necessarily from a specific film.

PRESS BOOK: Approximately 11 x 17 inches. The books, which served as advertising aids for print media and theaters, touted a magazine-like format for publicity, suggested story ideas, heralds, advance newspaper art, and photos of posters that could be ordered.

SCENE STILL: 8 x 10 inches, glossy black and white or color. Used for promotion in newspapers, magazines, and in theater lobbies. Much like lobby cards, scene stills were distributed in sets.

TITLE CARD: 11 x 14 inches. The first card in a lobby card set featuring poster-style artwork.

VIDEO ADVANCE POSTER: Sizes vary. Designed as a promotion for video stores to hype an upcoming release.

WINDOW CARD: 14 x 22 inches, full color and duotone. Though considered a poster, window cards were printed on heavier card stock and could not be folded. They included a four-inch blank border on top where the theater owner could write in dates and times of upcoming shows. The cards were then hung in drug store windows, barber shops, and other local venues as extra bits of advertising.

Unless otherwise noted, images in this book are from the author's private collection.

INDEX IMAGES

A. SCENE STILL. Pamela Duncan (19??–) and Dorothy Neumann (1914–94), *The Undead* (A.I.P., 1957). (JC Archives)

B. SCENE STILL. Ramsay Ames (1919–98), *Black Widow* (Republic, 1947). (JC Archives)

C. SCENE STILL. Marion Shilling (1910–) and Mae Busch (1891–1946), *Heart Punch* (Mayfair, 1932). (JC Archives)

D. PORTRAIT STILL. Esther Ralston (1902–94), *The Spy Ring* (Universal, 1938). (JC Archives)

E. SCENE STILL. June Havoc (1916–) and Dorothy Hart (1922–2004), *The Story of Molly X* (Universal, 1949). (JC Archives)

F. LOBBY CARD. Gloria Henry (1923–), *Yellow Fin* (Monogram, 1951).

G. FOREIGN MAGAZINE. Susan Hayward (1918–75), *Mon Film* (France, Nov. 1947).

H. SCENE STILL. Barbara Pepper (1912–69, middle) with Betty Blythe (1893–1972, left) and Dorothy Burgess (1907–61, right), *Girls in Chains* (PRC, 1943). (JC Archives)

I. LOBBY CARD. June Blair (1936–), *Hell Bound* (United Artists, 1957).

J. LOBBY CARD. Kathleen Turner (1956–), *Body Heat* (Warner Bros., 1981).

K. LOBBY CARD. Beverly Michaels (1927–), *Crashout* (Filmakers, 1955).

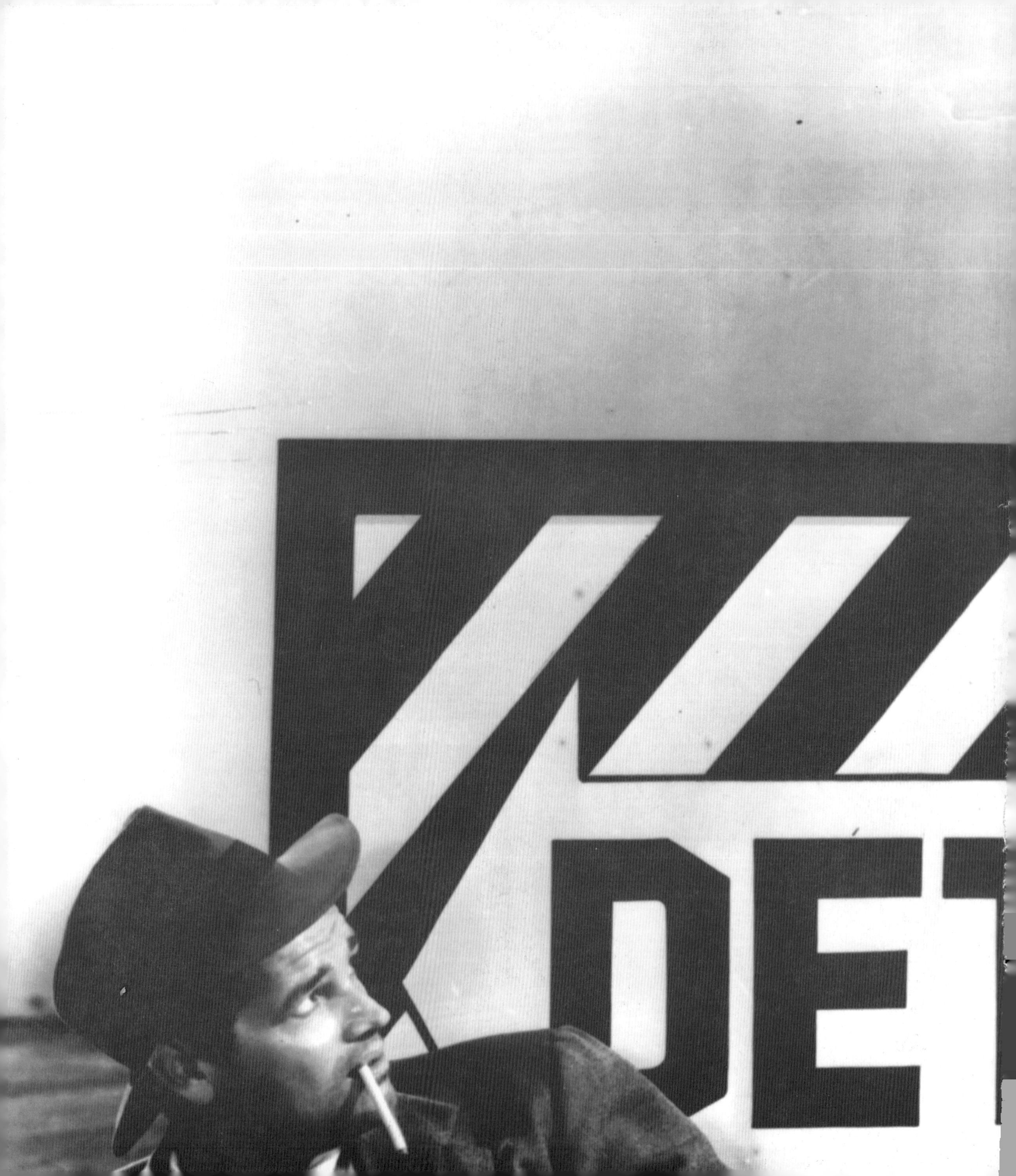